GOD'S BAILOUT

GOD'S BAILOUT

Principles of Kingdominion

Lemuel David Miller

"God's Bailout" Principles of Kingdominion
published by Judah, LLC Books & Publishing

Judah, LLC Books and Publishing
530 West River Road Suite 333
Jacksonville, Georgia 31544
Phone: 229-318-9341

First edition copyright © 2011 Lemuel David Miller

All rights reserved. No part of the publication may be reproduced, stored in a retrieval system, or transmitted, in any form or by any means, electronic, mechanical, photocopying, recording, or otherwise without written permission.

ISBN 978-0-9833794-1-6

Printed in the United States of America

Contents

Dedication 7

Introduction 9

Chapter 1: Keys to God's Bailout 11

Chapter 2: Keys to Kingdominion 23

Chapter 3: God's Miracle Bailout 33

Chapter 4: Bailout through Redemption 47

Chapter 5: Created to Manage 61

Chapter 6: Management Produces Multiplication 73

Chapter 7: The Government of God 89

Chapter 8: God's Security Program 103

Chapter 9: Ambassadors of Christ 117

Chapter 10: The Blessing of the Lord Brings Wealth 127

Chapter 11: Time to Rule and Dominate 139

IN CONCLUSION 161

Lemuel & Davonne Miller

Lemuel & Davonne Miller and Family (left to right) Saylah, Heather, Charlee, Sydney, Doug, Lemuel David, DaVonne, Amara, Presley, Jennifer, Joshua David, Rachel, Lemuel Davin

Dedication

I dedicate this work to my beloved grandparents, Tom and Ada Miller and Snowden and Rozella Farmer. They certainly grabbed hold of the *Davidic Covenant* that Isaiah referred to in Isa. 55:3 (KJV). *And I will make an everlasting covenant with you, even the sure mercies of David.*

This means the same things God promised David, He is promising us. What were these mercies? In 2 Sam. 7:16 God said to David, *your house* (meaning you and your future generations) *will be established forever.*

My grandparents, both the Millers and the Farmers, had 10 children each. My grandparents and most of their children, my parents included, are in heaven. All of those gone on loved and served the Lord.

There are three of my uncles on the Farmer side, Junior, Hairman, Robert and, and one daughter, Ruth, on the Miller side still with us. They all love Jesus with everything within them. Now, five generations later, we have dozens of ministers in our family who both worship and serve the same God of King David. Our household was, indeed, established forever!

My prayer is that my future generations will all come to know and have relationship with the same God my grandparents knew. Thank you God for my heritage and family!

Lemuel David Miller

Introduction

Do you realize your Heavenly Father loves you so much that He has a "Bailout" from the Kingdom of Heaven just for you? This "Bailout" is His gift to you, if you will simply receive. In this, the second book of a series of three concerning God's Bailout for your life, you will learn from God's word, you have been given the Keys (access) to the Kingdom of Heaven. This book will take you step by step, teaching you principles of how to operate in the supernatural realm of "Kingdominion."

What is "Kingdominion"? This is a word I made up a few years ago, which expresses to me what the terms "Kingdom of Heaven," "Kingdom of God," or "Government of God" represent. You see, the word "kingdom" has two parts. The first is "king," which means "ruler"—one who rules for life. Secondly, "-dom" comes from the word "dominion," meaning the power or right of governing and controlling; sovereign authority—which means, to control and dominate.

Do you realize that very few believers—if any—live in the authority God has given us to operate in? God wants you to rule, manage, and multiply the resources He has given you to work with—and when we do, His Bailout is provided.

Many believers think that if they can overcome sin, then one day they will experience an eternal home in Heaven. But few realize that Jesus has given them power and authority to rule every arena of their lives, here and now. Yes, power and authority over sickness, disease, depression, anxiety, worry, attacks against family, emotional trauma, and economic strife—as well as the ability to dominate your environment, which is the jurisdiction God Himself has given you to govern.

As you read, you will see how God taught me about Kingdominion principles from my parents' lifestyle and healing prayers, to hunting and fishing trips where the Holy Spirit taught me that I could take dominion over the deer of the woods and the fish of the sea. May I humbly submit: when you have faith to believe that you can literally catch a deer with your bare hands in the wild, you can believe that God still raises the dead!

CHAPTER 1

Keys to God's Bailout

"Blessed are the poor for theirs is the kingdom of heaven."

(Luke 6:20 KJV)

"BLESSED are the poor" does not mean you are blessed for being poor financially. God forbid! God wants you to have great wealth and prosperity for an abundant life. When the Word says "blessed are the poor," it means that the Kingdom is here to "bail you out" physically, mentally, spiritually, and financially.

> In Luke 4:18 (KJV): **"The Spirit of the Lord is upon Me, because He has anointed Me to preach the gospel to the poor ..."** [Emphasis added.]

The word "gospel" in scripture simply means "good news". Jesus is saying "I have good news for the poor: You do not have to be poor anymore; the Kingdom of Heaven, and all it has to offer, is available for even the poor. Come out from under the curse of poverty; I have something better for you. You do not have to be bound; you can be free. You do not have to live in poverty;

you can have the prosperity of the Kingdom of God, changing your poverty mindset."

Matthew 5:3 says it like this: **"Blessed are the poor in spirit." (KJV)**

When you study the culture and phraseology of the first covenant, the Old Testament, you frequently find that the true believers, the ones hard after God, are often referred to as "poor."

In Psalm 40:16-17, the Word gives us this illustration, as David writes,

"But may all who seek you rejoice and be glad in you; may those who love your salvation always say, 'the Lord be exalted!' Yet, I am poor and needy; may the Lord think of me. You are my help and my deliverer; o my God, do not delay."

(NIV)

Notice that David, the wealthiest of men and a king, still refers to himself as poor and needy. In comparison to the Kingdom of God, we can and must say with David that without Christ and the Kingdom, "I am poor and needy."

In Matthew 5, when Jesus uses the words "poor in spirit," he addresses those who realize their entire need. In following Jesus' example we should declare, "Lord, we are emptying ourselves of the pleasures of this sin-cursed kingdom to seek You and You alone. We will not worry about tomorrow but seek Your Kingdom, the Kingdom of Heaven."

Here is the foundation for the poor in spirit—the

meek, lowly, needy, and humble—to enjoy the Kingdom of Heaven, not just in another life somewhere in our future, but here and now!

You may ask, "How?" When we have truly built a relationship with Jesus, who is the Kingdom and all that the Kingdom represents, the so-called "poor in spirit" become rich in knowledge and begin to understand their true call and purpose. The hidden things and mysteries of scripture are revealed, and you realize that not only *shall* you have the Kingdom, you *already* have the Kingdom. His name is Yeshua, the Christ.

I believe Jesus was talking to the crowd—not only the twelve who claimed to be disciples—and He was saying, "Wherever you fit in this grand scheme of things, understand this: how blessed are the poor. Do not worry; I am the Kingdom, and I am with you."

Jesus teaches a powerful message of the Kingdom in Luke 6:3–12 (KJV), where He says,

> Blessed are the poor in spirit: for theirs is the kingdom of heaven. Blessed are they that mourn: for they shall be comforted. Blessed are the meek: for they shall inherit the earth. Blessed are they which do hunger and thirst after righteousness: for they shall be filled. Blessed are the merciful: for they shall obtain mercy. Blessed are the pure in heart: for they shall see God. Blessed are the peacemakers: for they shall be called the children of God. Blessed are they which are persecuted for righteousness' sake: for theirs is the kingdom of heaven. Blessed are ye, when men shall revile you, and persecute you, and shall say all manner of evil against you falsely, for my sake. Rejoice, and

be exceeding glad: for great is your reward in heaven: for so persecuted they the prophets which were before you.

What was Jesus actually saying?

How blessed are those who realize their need for Messiah, for the Kingdom of Heaven is *given* to them.
How blessed are those who mourn, for the Kingdom comforts.
How blessed are the meek, for they shall have the Kingdom here and now.
How blessed are they who hunger and thirst after righteousness. The Kingdom will fill them.
How blessed are they who show mercy; the Kingdom will give them mercy.
How blessed are the pure in heart; they will see the God of the Kingdom in all that they do.
How blessed are the peacemakers; they become sons and daughters of the Kingdom.
Even if you are mistreated and insulted for the Kingdom's sake, rejoice (jump for joy; celebrate), for great is your reward in the Kingdom.

To illustrate that the Kingdom of Heaven is for the "now" in your life, let's look at Mark 10:28–30 (NKJV)

Then Peter began to say to Him, "See, we have left all and followed You." So Jesus answered and said, "Assuredly, I say to you, there is no one who has left house or brothers or sisters or father or mother or wife or children or lands, for My sake

and the gospel's, who shall not receive a hundredfold now in this time—houses and brothers and sisters and mothers and children and lands, with persecutions—and in the age to come, eternal life."

Peter says, "We left all to follow You." We left our families, houses, lands, and businesses. "We have forsaken all."

Then the Kingdom speaks, and God's Bailout Program declares that whatever you gave for Kingdom's sake shall be returned to you **a hundredfold** in this lifetime, and in the one to come, you will receive eternal life. *Wow!* You can't get that at Chase or Wells Fargo—only in the Kingdom of Heaven!

A hundredfold! When? In this life; in the here and now. You do not have to wait for the time when you pass from this life to life eternal. No, this blessing is for this lifetime!

So the "Kingdom of Heaven" is Jesus' favorite subject and brings bountiful benefits, blessings, and promises that come to individuals who allow Jesus to rule in their hearts here and now! The Kingdom is God's "Bailout" for whatever the need in your life. There are no shortages in the "Kingdom of Heaven."

THE KINGDOM IS HERE

Matthew 10:7–9 (NKJV): **And as you go, preach, saying, 'The Kingdom of Heaven is at hand.' Heal the sick, cleanse the lepers, raise the dead, cast out demons. Freely you have received, freely give.**

Luke 9:1, 2 (NKJV): **Then He called His twelve disciples together and gave them power and authority over all demons, and to cure diseases. He sent them to preach the Kingdom of God and to heal the sick.**

Luke 9:11 (NKJV): **But when the multitudes knew it, they followed Him; and He received them and spoke to them about the Kingdom of God, and healed those who had need of healing.**

These verses prove that Jesus has given us power and authority over the kingdom of this world's cultures and curses. We have been given power to do what this world calls impossible. Cast out demons, heal the sick, cleanse disease, raise the dead, and provide for the needy. We must understand that God's word doesn't lie, nor fail. He said we can do these things, and because He said we can, we can. God is not limited; it is we who limit Him. Stop limiting God; start believing that what He said is true, and start demonstrating the Kingdom of God in you!

He said "Lay hands on the sick, and they shall recover." That means that every time we pray and lay hands on someone who is sick, they shall recover. Yes, it should happen every time, not just once in a while. Every time, because Yeshua said so! So if it is not happening every time, we should be questioning why not. Let's analyze and compare our triumphs and victories to our mistakes and failures, in order to be able to consistently demonstrate the power of the Kingdom of God.

DEAD RAISED TO LIFE

In the late 1970s and early 80s, Jesus was really teaching me about the authority of the Kingdom. In so doing, I began to see incredible miracles. One such miracle involved a fourteen-year-old boy named Rusty. Rusty was in a store in a mall when he got very sick. I had just met Rusty and knew nothing of his history. I could see by his pale complexion he didn't feel well, and I suggested he sit down, which he did.

After a few minutes, he was only getting worse, so I said, "Rusty, let me help you lie down." So a friend and I helped him to lie down on the floor, there in the store. Immediately, Rusty went into a very violent seizure. I heard someone shout, "Somebody call the paramedics!"

I had never seen anything like it. Rusty was convulsing and bucking like a wild horse, and I was concerned he might crack his head open on the floor. I quickly sat down and held his head in my lap and ask my friend to help keep Rusty from hurting himself. The two of us had our hands full.

Now, if you would, stop right here and look at those three verses again in Matthew 10 and Luke 9, above. Jesus has given us authority and power over sickness, disease, demons, and death—and, in Luke 10:19, even over **all** the power of the enemy.

> Luke 10:19 (KJV): **Behold, I give you the authority to trample on serpents and scorpions, and over all the power of the enemy, and nothing shall by any means hurt you.**

As my friend and I tried to help Rusty, I was praying to myself—I didn't want to offend anyone, as there

God's Bailout

were about forty people watching. "Lord," I thought, "I don't know what is going on here, so I need your direction."

As I held Rusty's head, my friend opened Rusty's shirt and loosened his pants, because the young man was having trouble breathing.

Suddenly I heard a hideous rumbling sound in Rusty's belly. I had never heard anything like it before. I happened to notice a lady looking through the large glass window from outside the store, and for some reason—it's amazing how the Spirit works—I shouted, "Are you his mother?" She nodded yes. I shouted, "Please come in!"

When she arrived, she sat at Rusty's feet without saying a word—just sat there. I thought, "This is weird; maybe she's in shock." But the real concern was Rusty. With the sound of this hideous rumbling going on in his stomach, I noticed him turning blue. His mother screamed "My God, he's turning blue!" I knew he was choking, so I tried to clear his airway.

I was praying more fervently, but after several minutes of Rusty being blue and unable to breathe, he died as I held his head in my lap.

I looked at my friend and asked for his assistance, as I was going to give CPR. I quickly moved to Rusty's side, tilted his head, opened his mouth, and leaned forward to give him mouth-to-mouth. Just then I heard the Spirit of the Lord speak. Tears come to my eyes even now, as I remember Him saying, "Command Satan to take his hands off of Rusty's life, in the name of Jesus Christ of Nazareth; then, plead the blood of Jesus!"

Suddenly I no longer felt considerate of others; I laid my right hand on Rusty's bare chest and shouted,

"Satan, I command you to take your hands off Rusty's life, in the name of Jesus Christ of Nazareth, and I plead the blood of Jesus!"

I heard the rumbling start again in Rusty's stomach, even though he was not breathing. I looked down and noticed a wave of red starting at Rusty's bare feet and moving up his body. It kept traveling up his body, and as it did the rumbling sound began to move with it, from his stomach to his chest and then to his throat. It was as though the wave of red had grabbed the rumbling and carried it up Rusty's body to his throat. Rusty began to violently cough expelling the demonic spirit that had taken his life and began to breathe normally.

He looked over at me and smiled, closed his eyes, and went to sleep. I shook Rusty by the shoulders and woke him. I said, "Rusty, Jesus has healed you, son, so I want you to say 'Thank you, Jesus.'"

Now, I didn't know whether Rusty knew Jesus personally or not, but he said, "Thank you, Jesus." I said, "Say it again," and he said "Thank you, Jesus." I said, "Rusty, say it one more time," and he said, "Thank you, Jesus!"

Rusty started to drop off to sleep again. So I shook him and said, "Rusty, wake up! Wake up!" When he did, I said, "I want you to say this: 'I plead the blood of Jesus.'" Rusty followed my directions and said "I plead the blood of Jesus." I said, "Say it again"; he did, and I said, "Again!" He said, "I plead the blood of Jesus!" I looked him in the eyes and said, "Now you can go to sleep." And right off to sleep he went.

Oh, I had myself a spell! I didn't care who was watching while I praised the Lord!

Wouldn't you know it, the paramedics showed up just then; they came hustling in and asked what was going on, as Rusty lay asleep. His mother, still sitting at Rusty's feet, said, "Ask him." She pointed to me. I said, "Rusty had a vicious seizure, and after several minutes of being as blue as your shirt"—blue indeed—"he died. But we prayed, and Jesus brought him back to life."

You should have seen the paramedics' faces. As they looked around the store, they saw all the people standing around, each one nodding, agreeing with what I had said.

One of the paramedics spoke: "If you don't mind, we're going to check him out anyway." I said, "Yes, sir, that is fine. As a matter of fact, I think you ought to take him to the hospital and let them run their tests. But what you and the doctors will find is absolutely nothing, because Jesus has performed a miracle." They looked at Rusty's mother. "Anything he says," she said, pointing to me.

Three days later, Rusty's mom and dad visited me, to tell me their son's story. They said, "Rusty was born having seizures. The doctors told us that because of the seizures, Rusty would never live to be a teenager, but he has survived to age fourteen. The doctors said that he would be on medication his entire life, and he has."

His mother said, "We did what you said, and they took Rusty to Tampa General Hospital, the hospital where he was born. They know him very well and have all his records. In the last three days, they have run every test you can imagine, and they cannot find anything wrong with him. They told us they cannot find any evidence that Rusty has ever had a seizure. Furthermore," she added, "whenever Rusty has a seizure, I always panic and pass out because of the fear of what the doctors had said about the seizures. But when I came into the store that day and sat at Rusty's feet, I somehow knew that this time everything was going to be alright."

I submit that what she experienced that day was the *Shalom* of God, the peace that passes understanding (Philippians 4:7)—and what the doctors couldn't provide, the "Provision of the Lord" did!

I ask the readers of this book to pause for a moment and say, "Thank you, Jesus," for Rusty's miracle. God deserves all the credit and all the praise!

THE KINGDOM OF GOD

Jesus taught that there is something very important to understand: the Kingdom of God doesn't come by observation.

> Luke 17:20–21 (NKJV): **"The kingdom of God does not come with observation; nor will they say, 'See here!' or 'See there!' For indeed, the Kingdom of God is within you."**

This means it is not coming as a temporal kingdom, with pomp and splendor. People always want to be able to see the blessings of the Kingdom with natural eyes, but your eyes are bound by an earth-cursed system. Jesus said, "You must see with your heart; don't you understand that **the Kingdom is within you**?"

The Kingdom is not something we have to wait for, nor is it something that we have to see with natural eyes. It is available to be within every believer who dares to believe.

Faith is what it takes to live and operate in the realm of the Kingdom of Messiah. When you move into this level of faith, you will see the Kingdom—indeed by faith—because it will work in you. Faith sees, and hope is the soil where faith grows. Fear, on the other hand, is blind and sees nothing. When faith is released, the Kingdom builds a throne in the heart of the believer. There Jesus, the King, establishes His throne in your heart—and that throne only comes to you when your heart is completely yielded to Christ, the King!But wait! Didn't Jesus say to Pilate in John 18:36, **"My Kingdom is not of this world"**? That's the entire point! It isn't of this world, so it cannot be bound by a world of limitation. How many times have you been told, "You can't do that"? You are living in the earth-cursed kingdom, but the blessed and limitless Kingdom of God is not bound or subdued in any way. This Kingdom operates in only one way—by faith! When you release your faith to believe that the Kingdom of Heaven is within you, its power and authority, given by Jesus, can take you to where the impossible is not only possible but even probable!

My parents continually demonstrated the power of the Kingdom as I grew up. Nothing seemed to shake their faith. When they prayed in the name of Jesus, they expected the Kingdom to move mightily. As I look back on the many miracles I've seen and enjoyed, due to the faith and prayers of John Ralph and Rosie Hazel Miller, tears of joy fill my eyes.

On one such occasion, I was sick with strep throat at about the age of six. My parents were my pastors, so they bundled me up and took me to church—even with my body burning with fever and my tonsils swollen until my throat was nearly shut. Some would say the only place I should have been was in a hospital. Thankfully, my parents didn't run to the doctor every time something went wrong. Instead of cabinets filled with drugs and medicines, we had the word of God, anointing oil, and the Kingdom. That night my dad anointed me with oil and had the believers pray. Immediately after their prayer, the fever left my body. I asked my dad whether I could testify, and he said yes.

With fresh strength in my body, I said, "Dad, Jesus has healed me. Before church, I could barely swallow, but now when I swallow, it's like a raw oyster going down!"

Ha! The power of the Kingdom in a six-year-old boy, never forgotten!

Chapter 2

Keys to Kingdominion

WE are meant to take dominion in the earth—"ruler domination." Jesus came to restore the Kingdom of God here on earth, and because of the finished work of the cross, as a believer, the Kingdom is inside of you! (Luke 17:21)

How do we take dominion—or, as we say, "ruler domination"? First of all, you must believe that by His sacrifice, Jesus has bought back everything that was lost due to the sin curse that came because of Adam's disobedience; and by redemption through His blood, we now have the right to dominate our environment.

> Genesis1:26 (NIV): **Then God said, "Let us make man in our image, in our likeness, and let them rule over the fish of the sea and the birds of the air, over the livestock, over all the earth, and over all the creatures that move along the ground."**

As an example, let me tell you a hunting story.

PASSING DOWN A FAMILY HERITAGE

In the early 1990's when my brothers John, Troy

and I started our Christian outdoor filming company, the Outdoor Journal, our theme was generationally passing down a family heritage. We accumulated literally hundreds of hours of footage hunting and fishing. On one such trip, my nephew Timothy and I were bow hunting for only one afternoon—poor scheduling—so I knew we really had to take dominion.

If you talk to anyone in this type of business, you will quickly learn just how hard it is to get footage of television-worthy quality. Many days and lots of hours are the norm, as the deer must come into the designated shooting lane at just the perfect angle, etc., etc. It is not an easy task, especially when hunting in the wild, as we were doing.

I can almost hear the question, "What do you mean *in the wild?*" The truth of the matter is that many of the outdoor hunting shows you see on television are filmed in high-fenced game pens. In a large pen, it is still not an easy task to get the proper footage, but it does cut down on the hours.

On my trip with Tim, because of the lack of time, we prayed and released our faith for great success. I declared that Tim would film me harvesting two deer back-to-back, and then I would film him shooting one.

Allow me to add, in Florida, where we were hunting, you can harvest two a day, per hunter—the most generous limit in the nation. So, yes, we were legal!

I placed our lock on stands in the tree, and we settled in together for the evening hunt. When you learn to take Kingdominion over your environment, hunting is all expectation. It is exhilarating! That evening was no different. After sitting in the tree for about thirty minutes, I heard a twig snap and whispered to Tim,

"Get the camera ready; here they come." Within five minutes, three deer walked in right to our tree, one in front of the other. I raised my bow as the lead deer looked back at the ones following I drew the bow and released the arrow, which found its mark. One down, two to go.

When the arrow was released, of course, the other deer heard the sound and ran off. I whispered to Tim, "Keep filming; they'll be right back." They had to come back, because they were under assignment.

I know this is hard to believe, and that is why for many years I didn't tell these stories—because those who have never taken "Kingdominion" over the fowl of the air, the beasts of the field, or the fish of the sea, simply do not believe this is possible. So, I can hear those questions: "You were deer-baiting with corn, weren't you?" Hear me when I say, absolutely not! No bait of any kind, nor gimmicks or game pens. Everything was totally natural and in the wild.

With both Tim and I in great anticipation, after about four or five minutes my second deer came in and stood broadside. Tim was ready, and I was ready, and evidently so was my deer. After harvesting deer number two and handing the bow to Tim, I took the camera. I said, "Okay, Lord, I thank you for these deer; now give Tim his shot." I turned the camera on and got into position, and here came the third deer—although he was coming in very tentative and "spooky" (paranoid). But little by little, he made his way to within twenty yards of our stand and turned broadside. Tim was ready and poised and according to the footage, he made a great shot on the third deer. But at the sound of the string being released, the deer nearly turned inside out, and in the process ducked the arrow. (Bow hunters call that "jumping the string.")

Tim and I both were disappointed, but after thinking over what had happened, we began to realize some very important principles.

First, God loves you to be specific? As a matter of truth notice I said "truth," not "fact" which is simply another example of being specific. I believe that facts change but truth never changes. The only truth is the Word of God, and that truth is forever settled. Thus, when facts do not align with the Word of God, the facts must change when the truth is applied. So, as a matter of truth, when I released my faith for that very successful afternoon hunt, I declared that we would take dominion over three deer. My declaration was that Tim would film me harvesting two deer, back-to-back, and then I would film him shooting one. In addition, after I had harvested my two deer, I gave God praise, saying, "Lord, I thank you for these deer. Now give Tim his shot."

These were the specifics: I declared that I would harvest two—which means they would end up in my freezer which they did—and then Tim would get a shot, or specifically, would shoot. There is a huge difference between the two declarations. "[Giving] Tim his shot" includes variables. Among those variables were paranoia for Tim's deer, while mine were calm—and "a shot," we found out the hard way, can mean a miss. On the other hand, "harvest" means reaping what you've sown!

After it was all said and done, we had a good laugh, and even now, many years later, we praise our Lord and Savior Jesus Christ for the power and authority of Kingdominion.

If you have Kingdominion, you must have the "Keys to the Kingdom."

Matthew 16:19 (NIV): **I will give you the keys of the Kingdom of Heaven; whatever you bind on earth will be bound in heaven, and whatever you loose on earth will be loosed in heaven**.

Christ's *kingdom is not of this world;* in Matthew 16:19, Jesus gives instructions *in things pertaining to the kingdom of God.* Jesus says, "I am giving you the Keys of the Kingdom of Heaven." Yes, Jesus was talking to Peter, but Peter represents every believer. Jesus declares, "As the master of the house, I give the keys to the Kingdom of Heaven to my stewards. These keys give you the power and authority—yes, the right—to open all the treasure chests of Heaven, and as a member of the household of God (Ephesians 2:19), you have the right to use the keys!"

God expects you to win, rule, manage, and dominate with success by authority of the Kingdom.

Allow me to ask you a question. Why should you rule? The answer is, God has given you the Keys to the Kingdom. Keys represent authority, legal rights, access. If the door is locked, without the right key, you have no access to enter.

Jesus says, "Here is what the keys to the Kingdom are." Whatever you bind on earth (in the earth-cursed kingdom of the earth) will be bound in heaven. And Jesus continues to say, "Whatever you loose on earth will be loosed in heaven." This binding and loosing is taking place in two places: number one, on earth, and number two, in heaven.

The word of God in Ephesians 2:2 teaches that Satan is the prince of the power of the air, and he dwells in the second heaven. Let me try to clarify. The first heaven is our atmosphere. The second heaven is somewhere between our atmosphere and the third heaven—known as the Heaven of Heavens, where God's throne is. The second heaven is also where the demonic powers of Satan dwell.

> Ephesians 6:12 (NKJV): **For we do not wrestle against flesh and blood, but against principalities, against powers, against the rulers of the darkness of this age, against spiritual hosts of wickedness in the heavenly places.**

Understanding how our enemy operates brings to light why Jesus has given us the keys to binding and loosing here on earth. God declares the heavens are mine and I have given the earth to mankind.

> Psalm 115:16 (NKJV): **The heaven, even the heavens, are the Lord's; But the *earth He has given to the children of men*.** [Emphasis added.]

If you have a need or desire, there is a key that will unlock the door and give you access to the blessing, deliverance, remedy, etc., of the Kingdom of Heaven.

BINDING THE WILL OF THE DEER TO MY WILL

Recently while deer hunting, I experienced an insight about these valuable Keys. I was slipping along through the woods and came to the edge of a field. "Slipping," as the term implies is quietly and carefully moving through the woods and when done properly, is a tedious, slow, time-consuming exercise—but the rewards are fabulous. As I stood at the edge of the field, hiding behind brush and trees, a doe walked into the field, about 175 yards away. She stopped and looked back over her shoulder. Knowing it was in the peak of the rut—breeding season for deer—by the way she was acting I fully expected the buck to be close behind, and I wasn't disappointed. But this particular doe wasn't quite ready to be courted closely, so she bolted and ran across the field.

I thought, "I must do something, fast!" Because I had no place to prop and steady for a shot, I quickly lay on the ground, but by the time I secured my rest, she was in the woods, with the buck close behind. It all happened so fast that I barely got a glimpse of the buck. But a little glimpse was all I needed to get my motor going.

I sat for a moment, a bit frustrated that I hadn't analyzed the situation and reacted faster. Then I had an unusual thought. So I said, in a quiet but audible voice, "I bind the will of the doe to my will and command her to come back to the field." In other words I was taking dominion over her will and binding it to mine.

What was the reasoning behind this lunacy? Being an avid hunter, I knew the buck would follow the doe wherever she went—kind of like me when I married my wife, DaVonne—so I didn't have to take dominion over two deer, only one.

Within seven or eight minutes, would you believe it? She had circled through the woods and came out into the field within about thirty-five yards from me—and who do you think was behind her? Well, the rest of the story is, my freezer is full.

The message I want you to receive is that most Christian believers only use the Keys to the Kingdom to bind demonic forces—and forget to use them in every other arena of life. But they work with any and all situations that you will ever face; don't you think it's time to start using this authority? My goodness, if it works while hunting, making a doe do what you declare, it surely will work in your family, finances, and circumstances! Just apply faith.

HOW TO APPLY THE KEYS WHEN FACED WITH EVIL

The keys are found in your binding the earth-cursed thing. Then, in turn, God Almighty binds the legal rights of Satan in the heavens so you can then loose the manifested power and presence of Kingdominion, ruler domination, in your life here on earth—thus causing the King of Heaven to loose and provide the answer you've released your faith to receive. Hallelujah!

Let me make this simple:

1. Bind the thing that is hindering here on earth; then God binds it in the heavens.
2. Loose the answer or remedy here on earth; then God looses it in the heavens.
3. Bind yourself to God's answer (remedy,

healing, deliverance, blessing, etc.) so you can keep it.

Always there are some who think they have no authority or power. If God's word is true, you are a people of authority and power.

Revelation 1:5–6 (KJV): **And from Jesus Christ, who is the faithful witness, and the first begotten of the dead, and the prince of the kings of the earth. Unto him that loved us, and washed us from our sins in his own blood, And hath made us kings and priests unto God and his Father; to him be glory and dominion for ever and ever. Amen.**

Notice that this scripture says that by the blood of Jesus, He has made us kings and priests. Where are we to be kings and priests?

Verse 5 says "the earth," and we are a people with supernatural power and authority here in the earth. Jesus said, "You are a king of the earth." Remember Psalm 115:16: **But the earth He has given to the children of men.**

The purpose of Jesus and the finished work of the cross were to restore kingship and dominion on earth. Kingship to the kings, who by the fall of man and the sin-curse, lost not only their kingship authority but also their priestly authority here on earth.

Jesus paid the ransom fee with His own blood, for the kidnapped kingly and priestly authority to be returned to believers. He was the Lamb slain from the foundation of the world. He shed His blood, a once-and-for-all payment, so we no longer have to offer blood sacrifices. His "finished work" (giving His life and accomplishing all He set out to redeem) bought back our legal rights to individually go to God; thus, kingship and dominion authority have been restored.

Do you realize you are no longer servants, but sons and daughters of the King, who has passed down a spiritual heritage of kingship—or should I say, "Kingdominion"—for you here on Earth? Friend, the devil has no business touching one hair on your head, or any resource God has given you, because Jesus, the King of Kings, has made you a king of the earth. We have authority and power even over the enemy of our souls.

Kings are accustomed to saying to one, "Go," and he will go; to another, "Come," and he will come (cf. Luke 7:8). Whatever they declare is for the good of the kingdom, not for selfish desire. When they speak, their words are carried out to the letter, because they are king!

POWER AND AUTHORITY OF A KING

> John 14:12 (NKJV): **Most assuredly, I say to you, he who believes in Me, the works that I do he will do also; and greater works than these he will do, because I go to My Father.**

You will do the same things Jesus did—and even greater. *Wow!* What did Jesus do? He healed all who came to Him—the deaf, dumb, blind, lame, diseased, sick, afflicted, and oppressed. He raised the dead, cast out demons, and everything in between. He fed thousands and provided what they couldn't.

How did Jesus do these great things?

John 3:34-35 (NLT): **For he is sent by God. He speaks God's words, for God's Spirit is upon him without measure or limit. The Father loves his Son, and he has given him authority over everything.**

The power of the Holy Spirit in Jesus' life was "without measure or limit." That's right: it gave Him all authority and power over all things. So why did Jesus offer you this awesome power? Jesus says, "I am going to the Father" (John 16:10). In other words, he is telling us, "I've done my part; now I desire that you should be My king representative on the Earth (Revelation 1:5, 6). I'm leaving you with My power to rule—so rule! And manage the resources that I am entrusting to you. I will leave you with an anointing without measure, enabling you to do even greater things than I have done (John 14:12)."

CHAPTER 3

God's Miracle Bailout

BROKEN BACK HEALED

BY the time my oldest daughter, Heather, was nine years old, she was a two-time world karate champion. In 1978, I had founded the Christian Karate Association (CKA), which had members literally around the world. Members were responsible for leading thousands of people to Christ.

Heather was a very active member of the CKA and was invited to do an exhibition at the World Karate Championship in 1984. At that time, I had retired as a two-time All-Around World Champion and was actively promoting tournaments and the CKA.

After arriving at the Omni Hotel in Miami, Florida, I attended a black belt meeting. There I had the privilege of witnessing to a good Baptist brother about the miracle-working power of God. Suddenly, the meeting was interrupted, as someone shouted, "Lem, Heather has fallen—it's serious!"

As you can imagine, I ran as fast as I could to my daughter. Heather had fallen from the second floor (mezzanine) to the main floor, which was made of marble. According to the doctor, along with a nurse of Jewish faith, Heather was paralyzed from the neck down.

The nurse who was a personal friend was crying as she explained that when Heather fell, she had landed with her right leg out in front and her left leg behind her, in what we term a hurdler's stretch position. She said the impact was so violent that the whiplash had caused the back of Heather's head to actually touch her bottom. The doctor had been keeping me from Heather, thinking it was for my good and hers, but I insisted on talking to her.

The doctor said, "Don't move her in any way; any movement could have serious consequences."

With paramedics on the way, I knelt beside my daughter and asked, "Do you believe that Jesus will heal you right now?"

Heather had been taught to believe that God can do the impossible, and she unhesitatingly responded, "Yes!"

Without thinking about what I was doing, I lay down over her body. The doctor went nuts. I said, "She's my daughter, and I'll take full responsibility."

Many days later, as I was recalling what had happened, I remembered that the prophet Elisha laid his body upon the body of a friend's dead son:

> 2 Kings 4:32–37 (NIV): **When Elisha reached the house, there was the boy lying dead on his couch. He went in, shut the door on the two of them and prayed to the LORD. Then he got on the bed and lay upon the boy, mouth to mouth, eyes to eyes, hands to hands. As he stretched himself out upon him, the boy's body grew warm. Elisha**

> turned away and walked back and forth in the room and then got on the bed and stretched out upon him once more. The boy sneezed seven times and opened his eyes. Elisha summoned Gehazi and said, "Call the Shunammite." And he did. When she came, he said, "Take your son." She came in, fell at his feet and bowed to the ground. Then she took her son and went out.

I had not pondered this action in advance but simply was led by the Holy Spirit to lie over Heather's body. I believe the same type of anointing is what brought her healing and life.

As I prayed, I felt the power of the Holy Spirit and allowed Him to pray through me. The power of the Kingdom began to pray through me, and suddenly, boldness came on me that I couldn't explain. I stood and said, "Heather, in the name of Jesus Christ of Nazareth, rise up and walk!"

The doctor began to say all kinds of things, but I looked at Heather as I said to the doctor, "Look at her countenance" There was such a drastic change, it was undeniable. I asked her, "Baby, where's your pain?"

She said, "Dad, I'm not hurting anymore."

I took her by the hand and asked, "Can you squeeze my hand?" The hand that she couldn't move before squeezed my hand. "Can you move your arms?" She did! "Heather," I said, "I'm going to help you sit up."

And when she sat up, she said, "Still no pain, Dad."

Now I was about to have a fit. I said, "Okay, let's stand up." As I helped her, I asked, "Any pain?"

She said, "Dad, Jesus healed me." And with that,

she lifted her leg—and, as a matter of fact, kicked me in the face!

Let me tell you, the Baptist brother and I did a jig right there at the Omni, and then a Jewish circle dance with the nurse! God is good!

Heather competed in the tournament that day, winning her third world championship, and performed her exhibition that night in the finals. Many of the greatest martial artists of the day were present. Chuck Norris, Bill "Super Foot" Wallace, Ed Parker, Robert Trias, and others, were all there that evening, watching the girl whom God healed! From these great martial artists, I heard comments like, "That was the greatest demonstration of martial arts ability I have ever seen." A nine-year-old girl, touched by the hand of the Lord. The Kingdom of Heaven came to the Omi Hotel in the form of divine intervention!

Colossians 1:12 (NLT): **"always thanking the Father, who has enabled you to share the inheritance that belongs to God's holy people, who live in the light."**

As believers we have an inheritance, we are heirs of God and joint or co-heirs with Jesus:

Romans 8:17 (NIV): **Now if we are children, then we are heirs—heirs of God and co-heirs with Christ.**

What Jesus has, we too can have. We need not be bound to an earth-cursed kingdom, but because of faith we can be translated from the earth cursed kingdom to a Kingdom out of this world—and even experience His Divine Health!

DIVINE HEALING A FORM OF GOD'S BAILOUT PROGRAM.

Did you know that fear, stress, and negative thoughts can open the door for your life to be filled with sickness and disease? Medical science is declaring that as much as 95% of sickness and disease results from stress. Let me show you God's Bailout Plan for your health.

> James 5:15 (KJV): **And the prayer of faith shall save the sick, and the Lord shall raise him up; and if he have committed sins, they shall be forgiven him.**

This word "save," in the Greek, actually means much more than even eternal life. It means health, wholeness, prosperity, and peace, as well as eternal life. You see, when you get saved (born again, turning in repentance to trust your life to God), at that moment, healing is also available, and prosperity is available. The peace (*shalom*) of God should, at that moment, come into your life, because that is what the Kingdom of God offers. But we haven't been taught all of the truth, so we're walking around bound to things that should never be binding us.

Miracle in the Vestibule

Frankie Carpenter who is one of my church members, had been very ill for several days, spending most of her time at doctors' offices. They were trying to get her to a specialist in Macon, Georgia, which is about an hour and a half from where she lived. What you are about to read is Frankie's and my story of a divine encounter.

At China Hill Christian Church we have our midweek service on Tuesday nights. That particular Tuesday, the Glory of the Most High God had been ushered in by the praise of the people—so much so that during the praise, people voluntarily began to come to the altar, seeking God.

I left the piano while the praise continued, and began to minister to the ones at the altar. Suddenly the sanctuary doors flew open, and Lucy Furney—a member and deaconess of the church—screamed, "Pastor! Frankie has fallen and passed out in the foyer!"

Ronny Barron, one of my Elders and I quickly ran to Frankie's aid. When we arrived, she was face-down. Ronny got to her first and began to roll her onto her back. She was purple, cold as ice, with the blood coagulating in her neck. We were already praying when we determined that there was no breath, pulse, or life.

I laid my right hand on her head and rebuked the spirit of death, and then loudly declared, "Frankie, you shall not die but live and declare the works of the Lord!"

Instantly, Frankie blew out a puff of air and then took a breath—but the enemy continued to fight. Her breathing continued only sporadically.

By that time, everyone had come to the foyer, and all were praying with one accord. Some were kneeling, others standing or pacing, and some were crying—but all were concerned.

I moved and lay face-down on the floor above Frankie's head as she lay on her back with both of my hands under her head to tilt it properly so her breathing would be easier. As I did, I placed the right side of my face by her left ear nd began to speak the word of God to her spirit. The scriptures were rolling out of me in the power of the declared Word. And whenever I made a declaration, I could hear the saints around us agreeing in prayer and declaring the same. Tears were flowing as the saints' faith began to build, refusing to settle for anything less than a miracle.

Henry Batts, a young state trooper and powerful man of God, began to give CPR, with the aid of Sister Wilma and my daughter Rachel, as I continued to hold Frankie's head and speak the word of God to her.

> Psalm 107:20 (KJV): **He sent his word, and healed them, and delivered them from their destructions.**

I've seen a number of deaths in my ministry. I can tell you from experience that because the blood had already coagulated—made a pocket of blood—in Frankie's neck, she must have been dead for ten to fifteen minutes. Her body temperature was as cold as if she had been refrigerated. During this time, Frankie had an out-of-body experience. I have asked her to write her story in her own words.

Frankie's Story

On September 30, my pulse had dropped to 40. I thought "This can't be," so I took it again, but it was the same. I was so tired that I went to sleep but awoke feeling like I needed to be at church.

Since the service had already started, I texted my

daughter Anna and asked her if she would come get me as soon as praise and worship were over. She said she would, but I could feel the Holy Spirit urging me not to wait. I don't remember getting in the car and driving to my mother's house, but I do remember going in and seeing her on the phone talking to my brother. I asked her to hang up and take me to church. When we got there, I asked her to pull up and get me as close to the front door of the church as possible.

The next thing I saw was Lucy Furney bending over me and then opening the sanctuary door and screaming, "Pastor, Frankie's passed out!" I know I was face-down on the floor, but I could see vividly. I was having an out-of-body experience.

I remember seeing Wilma Conner on my right side and thinking that she was breaking my ribs! Her husband, Charles, was at my feet. I also saw Tom Jackson, our youth pastor. Henry Batts was on my left, and I knew there was someone else there but didn't know it was Rachel Miller until Anna told me later on. My pastor, Lemuel Miller, was lying on his stomach above my head. He had his hands under my head, and at one point, I felt his cheek next to my cheek and felt his tears, although these were not desperate tears. Sometimes when he prays in the Spirit, there will be tears on his cheeks.

I could see people all around me praying. Some were by my side, some were on their knees, and others were standing. But all were in one accord. One of the things I saw, that I still get very emotional about, was seeing my daughter Anna and hearing her screaming, "Mama, Mama! That's my mama!" She was surrounded by people praying for her also.

Then my daddy, who had gone to heaven several

years ago, came to me there in the vestibule. All I could see was his face, and I never saw him open his mouth, but he told me that he had been praying for me. He told me that my mama needed me. He said that God had work for me to do and that I had to go back.

I don't remember much of anything else for the next three days, only bits and pieces—although every once in a while God reveals things to me that happened that night. He told me that the tears on pastor Lem's cheeks were His tears, tears of the Holy Spirit, and that He was cleansing me and making me whole. He said that He came to me in the form of my daddy that night because He knew I would listen to him. Another time, He revealed to me that the tears I felt on my cheek that night were the kiss of the Holy Spirit.

I don't know whether Lucy was wearing yellow that night or if God was shining on me, but sometimes I have a memory of yellow. I was told that Pastor Lem and Ronnie Barron were the first to get to me after Lucy found me, and when they turned me over, I was purple and ice-cold to the touch.

It was estimated that I was probably gone for ten to fifteen minutes. After the paramedics took me to the hospital, I had an emergency heart cath in Macon, and my cardiologist said that my arteries were 100% clear and I had the heart of an eighteen-year-old.

This one thing I am sure of: God met me in the vestibule at China Hill Christian Church!

Pastor Lem said that when he came through the sanctuary door; he felt the spirit of death. He began rebuking it. He started declaring that I would "live and not die and would declare the works of the Lord." Praise God! Everyone who was at the church started praying the same thing, and here I am—still alive and declaring what God has done! *Praise the Lord!*

—Frankie

RESURECTION POWER OF THE HOLY SPIRIT

Allow me to point something out about Frankie's experience. She said that God revealed to her that the tears on my cheeks were **God's tears, tears of the Holy Spirit, and that He was cleansing her and making her whole.**

Remember that the Word says in Luke 17:21, "the Kingdom of God is within you!" It was indeed the Kingdom, which is the Holy Spirit that raised Frankie from the dead.

Romans 8:11 (KJV): **But if the Spirit of him that raised up Jesus from the dead dwell in you, he that raised up Christ from the dead shall also quicken your mortal bodies by his Spirit that dwelleth in you.**

Proverbs 3:5 (KJV): **"Trust in the Lord with all your heart. Lean not to your own understanding."**

Let me say again, "Lean not to your own understanding." Why? If we go by our own understanding, we will get it wrong. Remember, we need to repent for wrong patterns of thinking, such as: "God allowed me to be raped, molested, misused, and abused." May I say to you emphatically, no, He did not!

Just like you cannot make decisions for any of your

family members, God never interferes with human beings' free-will choices. Sadly, people may choose to do bad things, and sometimes others are innocent victims. This is why bad things happen to good people. This is the whys and wherefores of the tragedy of 9/11. Very bad people made bad choices and took the lives of thousands of innocent victims.

Some have asked, "Where was God?" on that day. The same place He was when bad people crucified His Son. He was there, in tender love and compassion for every scream, every tear, every wound, and every death.

If you have been traumatized by circumstances, allow God to redeem your trauma. Here is the key: God doesn't allow bad things, but through this earth-cursed kingdom, when evil occurs, the most important thing is for you to allow God to fix it. God wants to bail you out of the trauma, and the health problems that most likely were caused by the trauma in your life. Please release your faith to believe that God wants you to be healed, delivered, and completely set free.

My parents taught me, as a child, to believe God for anything. They always said "God loves you and will do the impossible for you." God taught me much about the Kingdom through healing experiences, allowing me to see His miracle-working hand in my life over and over again.

I was healed of fevers. Because of the prayers and faith of my parents, those fevers never had a chance to break, or for me to sweat them off; they simply disappeared. I fell from a roof when I was nine. I fell flat on my back, landing on a hammer and a two-by-four board. I remember that when I hit the ground, the pain was excruciating. I tried to get up and couldn't. My father and a member of our church got to me immediately, telling me not to move, as they knew the possibility of my back being broken. Dad began to pray for me as the church member ran to call for an ambulance. By the time I arrived at the hospital, my pain had left, and the doctors couldn't find anything wrong. My dad was a powerful man of God, with extreme faith.

Another time, after my dad had gone to be with the Lord, my kidneys shut down, and I was bleeding internally. The doctors never discovered why. As my mother drove to the hospital, she prayed, telling my kidneys to function as God intended and commanding the bleeding to stop. God came into the room and healed me. Instantly, my kidneys started working, the bleeding stopped, and the high fever I had disappeared. Thank You, Jesus!

What I am trying to tell you is, this stuff works!

II Peter 1:3 says, **"He has given to us all things that pertain to life and godliness."**

This means that whatever you need, it's available. It has been given, given, given to us the believers. What has been given? *All things* that pertain to the abundant life promised by God Himself.

How do we maintain these blessings?

Carry out the will of the Father! Jesus did. There are fourteen people groups listed in the scripture passages below that we, as kings of the earth, are commanded to minister to:

Matthew 25:34–36 (NIV): **Then the King will say to those on the right, "Come, you who are blessed by my Father, inherit the Kingdom prepared for you from the foundation of the world. For I was <u>hungry</u>, and you fed me. I was <u>thirsty</u>, and you gave me a drink. I was a <u>stranger</u>, and you invited me into your home. I was <u>naked</u>, and you gave me clothing. I was <u>sick</u>, and you cared for me. I was <u>in prison</u>, and you visited me."** [Emphasis added.]

Romans 12:20 (NLT): **Instead, do what the Scriptures say: "If your <u>enemies</u> are hungry, feed them. If they are thirsty, give them something to drink, and they will be ashamed of what they have done to you."** [Emphasis added.]

Isaiah 58:7, 8 (NLT): **I want you to share your food with the hungry and to welcome <u>poor</u> wanderers into your homes. Give clothes to those who need them, and do not hide from <u>relatives</u> who need your help. If you do these things, your salvation will come like the dawn. Yes, your healing will come quickly. Your godliness will lead you forward, and the glory of the LORD will protect you from behind.** [Emphasis added.]

Deuteronomy 14:29 (NLT): **Give it to the <u>Levites</u>, who have no inheritance among you, as well as to the <u>foreigners</u> living among you, the <u>orphans</u>, and the <u>widows</u> in your towns, so they can eat and be satisfied. Then the LORD your God will bless you in all your work.** [Emphasis added.]

Malachi 3:5 (NLT): **"At that time I will put you on trial. I will be a ready witness against all sorcerers and adulterers and liars. I will speak against those who cheat <u>employees</u> of their wages, who oppress widows and orphans, or who deprive the foreigners living among you of justice, for these people do not fear me," says the LORD Almighty.** [Emphasis added.]

I recommend that you study all of these passages.

Fourteen Groups of People: The hungry, the thirsty, strangers, the naked, the sick, the imprisoned, enemies, the poor, relatives, Levites (priests), foreigners, orphans, widows, and employees.

We demonstrate the kingdom when we minister to these, changing the hearts and minds of unbelievers with a demonstration of unconditional love! Every time you minister to the needy, the blessings of the Kingdom come to you.

Isaiah 58:8 (NKJV): **… your healing will come quickly. Your godliness will lead you forward, and the glory of the LORD will protect you from behind.**

Talk about being blessed! You will walk in great

power and anointing. If you need healing, it will come very quickly. You will walk in such favor that your rights will precede you, and the glory of the Lord will guard your back. You are protected by God Himself. Do you understand that when you trust God, God has got your back! Hallelujah!

CHAPTER 4

Bailout through Redemption

"In the earth-cursed kingdom"

THERE are laws that never change in the earth-cursed kingdom. Examples include the law of gravity, the changes of the seasons, the fact that the sun rises in the east and sets in the west—and as surely as you live, you will die.

In Genesis 3:17–19 (NIV), we read,

> To Adam he said, "Because you listened to your wife and ate from the tree about which I commanded you, 'You must not eat of it,' cursed is the ground because of you; through painful toil you will eat of it all the days of your life. It will produce thorns and thistles for you, and you will eat the plants of the field. By the sweat of your brow you will eat your food until you return to the ground, since from it you were taken; for dust you are and to dust you will return."

God said to Adam, "cursed is the ground because

of you." Because Adam was disobedient, from that day forward if he was to eat, he would have to work hard for his food, and the toil would be painful. The ground was now cursed so that, from then on, it would produce thorns and thistles—signs of poverty. By the sweat of our brow, we must work for food. And by the way—as we were created from the dust, to the dust we must return.

The Ransomed Power of the Blood of Christ!

Jesus ransomed everything that was lost due to the sin curse:

Isaiah 53:5 (KJV): **But he was wounded for our transgressions, he was bruised for our iniquities: the chastisement of our peace was upon him; and with his stripes we are healed.**

Let's look at scripture and find out what was ransomed (brought back to the original state) by Jesus.

HIS SWEAT BECAME AS GREAT DROPS OF BLOOD (Luke 22:44)

What did Jesus ransom? He ransomed discipline and willpower. By a choice of our will, we can now say no to sin and yes to God, because willpower has been given back to the believer.

Luke 22:44 (KJV): **And being in an agony he prayed more earnestly: and his sweat was as it were great drops of blood falling down to the ground.**

Genesis 3:19 (NIV): **By the sweat of your brow you will eat your food until you return to the ground, since from it you were taken; for dust you are and to dust you will return.**

The question is, how did Jesus ransom willpower for believers? By becoming our sacrifice and giving His blood. The first place Jesus gave His blood was in a garden—and that is no accident. When He shed His blood in the garden of Gethsemane, He bought back, paid in full, something that was lost many years before in the Garden of Eden. Remember, in the Garden of Eden, Adam had it all. He had dominion over all the earth. He walked with God in the cool of the evening. There was no sickness or disease, and Adam was a genius—having proved it by naming all life forms. God had told Adam, "It's all yours, except one tree."

God has always had something that is sacred to Him that He keeps just for Himself, and in the Garden of Eden, it was the Tree of the Knowledge of Good and Evil. Later God said, "Don't touch the tithe; it belongs to me." God said the tithe always belongs to Him, and if we take it, we rob Him. He also said, "Don't touch My anointed." But first it was the Tree of the Knowledge of Good and Evil—and God said, don't touch it!

Eve ate first, and the Bible says she was beguiled—tricked. But because Adam was the covering of Eve, the curse came through Adam (Genesis 3:17), whom the Bible says *willfully* disobeyed God.

I hope you understood what I just wrote. Adam's first sin was *not* eating the fruit of the Tree of the Knowledge of Good and Evil. Rather, it was his failure to protect his wife from temptation. Adam was her covering! When

Adam disobeyed, he was saying, "Father, not your will but mine be done." So sin entered through one man to all mankind.

But just as sin entered all of humanity through one man, through one man shedding his own precious blood—Jesus—sin is redeemed for all who will believe. The first Adam surrendered the willpower of all mankind when he said, "My will be done—I choose to eat of this tree. Yes it is disobedience, but it is still my will."

It's very evident that, because of the curse of sin, many have lost all their willpower. Because of a lack of willpower, many are bound to drugs, alcohol, sex, and other addictions.

But, watch this; in the Garden of Gethsemane, Jesus, while praying, was waging a battle between His flesh and His soul (His mind, emotions, and will).

> Luke 22:42-44 (NKJV): **... saying, "Father, if it is Your will, take this cup away from Me; nevertheless *not My will, but Yours, be done.*" Then an angel appeared to Him from heaven, strengthening Him. And being in agony, He prayed more earnestly. Then His sweat became like great drops of blood falling down to the ground.** [Emphasis added.]

Listen to the flesh: "Father, if there be some other way, let this cup pass from me." In other words, "I don't know how much more of this pain I can take. Please, let's find another way." But let's also, listen to the soul: **"yet not My will, but Yours, be done."**

Willpower was redeemed by the blood of Jesus Christ!

Luke 22:44 (NKJV): **And being in agony, He prayed more earnestly. Then His sweat became like great drops of blood falling down to the ground.**

Doctors say that most die from a heart attack before this phenomenon can take place. But if they don't die, the fear, anxiety, tension, and rapid increase of blood pressure may cause the blood vessels under the skin to burst, and the blood will pour forth from the pores of the skin.

When Jesus surrendered to the will of the Father and His sweat became great drops of blood, at that moment—for every drug addict, every alcoholic, every person bound by habits, hang-ups, and vices—Jesus purchased back for us *willpower!*

Willpower is the discipline in our lives to say, "Not my will but thine be done." What this means is, you don't have to be a junkie; your willpower has been redeemed by the blood of the Lamb of God.

Then, how do we move from our will to His will? Allow Jesus to redeem your willpower, by faith in His blood sacrifice. He paid the price!

Isaiah 53:5: **By His stripes *we are healed!***

When they hung Jesus on the whipping post, they beat Him with a cat-o'-nine-tails, and He took thirty-nine lashes from a cat-o'-nine-tails which were for our healing.

Several years ago the American Medical Association Journal published an interesting article which traced all the world's diseases to thirty nine root sources.

Jesus was whipped and ripped open by the cat-o'-nine-tails, and every time He took a stripe, *blood* gushed forth. His stripes are what ransom us from sickness and disease: "For by His stripes, we are healed."

The Bible says we are redeemed by the blood of the Lamb. The word "redeemed" means not just "saved" or "forgiven sins" but also "ransomed," as if we had been kidnapped.

The word "ransomed," in turn, in the Hebrew culture means, "brought back to the original state." Have you ever wondered what is available to you as God's child? Just go back and look at what God had given Adam before sin. In the Garden of Eden, was there any sickness? *No!* But since the sin curse, sickness and disease have run rampant. But by the stripes of Jesus, we are healed. Thus, there is *no* reason to be sick, because we are redeemed by the blood! By His stripes, you have been ransomed from all sickness and disease. When a sniffle comes, stop it there and give no place to the devil. Don't say, "I'm getting a cold." No! Say, "Hey, devil, you have no legal rights, so, *get away*, in the name of Jesus Christ!"

CROWN OF THORNS: PROSPERITY BROUGHT BACK TO THE ORIGINAL STATE

In Isaiah 53:1–5, we find that Jesus was wounded for our transgressions (our rebellion). By the wounds he suffered, watch how He took away our poverty.

The soldiers placed a crown of thorns on Jesus' head. When they pressed those three-and-a-half-inch thorns into His brow, blood—precious blood—was shed. Now remember, it is Jesus' blood that redeems and ransoms, to take back what has been kidnapped and return it to where it belongs, to its original state.

Was there poverty in the Garden of Eden? *No!* God is not a poverty God; therefore Christianity ought not to be bound by poverty. When Adam and Eve fell, God came to Adam and said, "No longer are you going to live in abundance; you will only earn a living by the sweat of your brow." Then the land was cursed with thorns and thistles.

> Genesis 3:18 (KJV): **Thorns also and thistles shall it bring forth to thee; and thou shalt eat the herb of the field.**

Come with me to Calvary, where the very symbol of poverty, thorns, are made into a crown and placed on the brow of the second Adam, Yeshua the Christ. From His brow flowed precious blood—and you and I are ransomed by the blood of the Lamb of God (Jesus) from the curse of poverty. I hope you'll get this. Jesus has already redeemed us from the curse of poverty! And because of His blood sacrifice you have the right to command this curse to be broken off your life. I admonish you to make the following declaration.

Declaration to break the curse of poverty:

"Satan, in the name of Jesus, poverty has lost its legal rights, due to the ransoming power of the blood of the Lamb of God. I have faith in God's ability to bail me out of and set me free from the curse of poverty and bless me to become financially secure in the Kingdom of God!"

NAILED HANDS: JESUS BOUGHT BACK OUR AUTHORITY

Hands (*yad* in Hebrew) are a symbol of authority. When Adam fell, Satan became the Prince of the Power of the Air. But Jesus, when His hands were nailed to the tree and His blood came streaming down, ransomed our authority back to its original state.

After His resurrection, Jesus said, "I am sending you another comforter" (John 14:16), the very Spirit of God, living in us. *We must use this authority.* God is in *us!* Now Jesus says that when this happens, we'll have the authority to cast out devils, and lay hands on the sick and watch them recover (Mark 16:17, 18). But He also warns us to lay hands on no man suddenly (1 Timothy 5:22) meaning there is an authority released, an impartation, when your hands touch someone so, make sure if you lay hands on someone, you are being led by the Holy Spirit.

When Jesus bled from His hands, His blood redeemed what had been lost in the first Adam: the right-handed blessing, the very authority of God, the blessing of full inheritance. With this ransomed authority, we can now live according to the word of God in Deuteronomy chapter 28.

Deuteronomy 28:8 (NKJV): **The Lord will command the blessing on you in your storehouses and in all to which you *set your hand*, and He will bless you in the land which the Lord your God is giving you.**

NAILED HIS FEET: JESUS BOUGHT BACK OUR SURE FOUNDATION

The wounds of Jesus' feet, as they were nailed to the cross, caused blood to flow that ransomed us foundationally. These wounds have returned to us the original privilege of being able to walk and commune with God personally. God walked with Adam in the cool of the evening communing with God the Father daily; now we can walk with Him and talk with Him 24/7 because Jesus not only restored our ability to walk with God but also ransomed dominion to rule with power and authority which is demonstrated in the following verse.

> Hebrews 2:8 (NKJV): **You have put all things in subjection** *under his feet.* [Emphasis added.]

"Under your feet" means that we have the power to subdue all things created by God's hands.

> Psalm 8:6 (KJV): **Thou madest him to have dominion over the works of thy hands; thou hast** *put all things under his feet.* [Emphasis added.]

With this magnificent power comes supernatural authority to claim. It is time to claim what you want, claim what you need—yes, claim what has already been given to you!

> Deuteronomy 11:24 (KJV): **Every place whereon the** *soles of your feet* **shall tread shall be yours**. [Emphasis added.]

Literally taking God at His Word

My wife and I wanted to buy a parcel of forty acres of land, even though we did not have the money for it. It was a beautifully wooded piece of property, and I had a dream of being able to high-fence so I could raise white-tailed deer. I'll never forget the day I went and walked the boundary markers of the land, declaring the Word of the Lord. Every step I took, I said, "Every place the soles of my feet tread shall be mine." I walked the property believing that if God said it, He would do it and bring it to pass. Within a few days, the property was ours, and I was enabled to enjoy my deer farm!

In addition, we need to recognize that Jesus is our foundation.

Ephesians 2:20 (KJV): **And are built upon the foundation of the apostles and prophets, Jesus Christ himself being the chief corner stone;**

With Jesus as our chief corner stone we become so grounded that in our standing on Jesus, our sure foundation, we can most assuredly declare; we shall not be moved!

PIERCED HIS SIDE TO HEAL THE BROKEN HEART

As Jesus hung on the cross a soldier took a spear and drove it into the side of Jesus and out of that wound came blood and water (John 19:34). Medical science states, when blood and water came out, it were a physical sign of a broken heart.

What caused Jesus' heart to break? The emotional and physical stress of Him taking on Himself the sins of the world, so squeezed the blood in the heart of Jesus that internal pressure rose to bursting strength. In other words, Jesus' broken heart, I believe, was caused due to His love for a sin cursed world. As He bore our sins He also fulfilled prophesy (Isaiah 61:1) and felt the infinite weight and coldness of your sins and mine.

> Luke 4:18 (KJV): **The Spirit of the Lord is upon me, because he hath anointed me to preach the gospel to the poor; he hath sent me to *heal the brokenhearted*, to preach deliverance to the captives, and recovering of sight to the blind, to set at liberty them that are bruised.** [Emphasis added.]

I know there are many people who have had tragic things happen to them. We all have experienced a broken heart! But Jesus ransomed your broken heart and wants to redeem it to its original state. Let me tell you, the hurts and traumas of your past can be redeemed right now, this very minute, if you're willing to trust Jesus. I want to pray a prayer with you. What I have noticed is, every time I pray this prayer, 100% of the time, the broken heart is healed.

Your hurt has left a wound in your heart. But Jesus says, "I've redeemed the brokenhearted, through the pouring out of my blood, if you dare to believe." Not only will He heal the brokenhearted, He will heal the wound—the memory—deliver you from your past, and show you your future! So now, if you will, please pray this prayer and believe Jesus is going to heal your heart right now!

Prayer for your broken heart

Heavenly Father, I purpose and choose to forgive _____ [person's/people's name] who [hurt me; specific trauma; broke my heart]. I forgive them and ask You to cancel their sins and obligations to me. Lord, forgive me for any resentment or bitterness that I have toward [the person(s)]. I release myself from this bitterness.

In the name of the Lord, Jesus Christ, I cancel all of Satan's power and authority over me in this memory, and I command the all fear and trauma to leave me now and never return.

Holy Spirit, please come and heal my heart. Lift the shock and trauma off my nervous system, and heal my synaptic connections. Cleanse my mind from all smells, pictures, sounds, touch, taste, physical pain, and feelings that have caused a broken heart in me. I ask that You correct my wrong patterns of thinking by changing the grooves and chemical balance of my mind. Father, I also ask that You give me the mind of Christ, and by the revelation of Your Holy Spirit, please tell me Your truth.

Take a moment to pause and listen, as the Holy Spirit speaks to you about your heart. When He points out a hurt, trauma etc. by reminding you through memory, take time to pray for each memory and receive your healing.

BRUISED FOR OUR INIQUITIES: REDEEMED FROM GENERATIONAL CURSES AND GUILT

Exodus 34:7 (KJV): **... keeping mercy for thousands, forgiving *iniquity* and transgression and sin by no means clearing the guilty,** *visiting the iniquity of the fathers upon the children and the children's children to the third and the fourth generation.*
[Emphasis added.]

Transgression is your rebellion against God and sin is the offences against God and His word. The word being His covenant, rules, regulations also known as commandments.

Iniquity is that sin tendency in your life that is passed down from generation to generation. You are bent toward it; you lean to it. It is the sin in your life that keeps returning—the sin you keep praying to get rid of, that is constantly a battle for you.

Iniquity can also be what your parents, grandparents and even great grandparents have passed down to you that you struggle with? Furthermore, what are you passing to your children that you struggle with, and now they face the same struggles?

Isaiah 53:5 says, "He was bruised for our iniquities." *Bruising is bleeding from the inside.* Iniquity is also from the inside, and is bondage. It is the sin you are bound too, the one you can't seem to shake; and it is this bondage that is often—though not always—passed generationally.

When Jesus gave His life, He ransomed us from iniquity. "He was bruised"; Jesus bled on the inside. Iniquity is our wicked weakness on the inside.

Jesus bled on the inside so that every generational weakness, tendency, sickness, and disease would be broken and redeemed by His blood! If you have truly received this into your spirit, you will, from this very moment, be able to say, "Satan, you're not going to win this battle! You have no legal right to punish me for my iniquities or the iniquities of my ancestors! Jesus was bruised for our iniquities. My iniquity is ransomed by the Blood of the Lamb!"

Prayer to break iniquity, individual and generational:

> Heavenly Father and most holy God, I come to you today, humbly, in my heart asking you to cleanse and sanctify me from all iniquity, transgression, and sin in my life. Please forgive me of all bitterness and unforgiveness that I have cherished toward anyone whom I have sinned against or who has sinned against me. I ask you to forgive, cleanse, and break the curse of iniquity in my life and the lives of my future generations.
>
> I repent of my sins, iniquities, and transgressions, and according to your Word, confess the sins and the iniquities of my ancestors, going back to Adam.
>
> I know from Your Word, Father, that Jesus, your only begotten Son, died on Calvary's cross to ransom me and my family from all curses. Right now, Father, I ask you in the name of Jesus Christ to ransom me from the curse of

fear, self-pity, self-bitterness, the curse of the illegitimate, and all other curses that may be in my life and the lives of my family. I nail the iniquities, transgressions, and sins of myself and my ancestors to the cross, going all the way back to Adam.

In the name of Jesus Christ, our Lord, I declare that the tormentors [evil spirits] have no authority or power in my life or the lives of my family, because we have been freed by the blood of the Lamb of God. Satan, you have lost your power of bondage over me, in Jesus' name.

Father God, please deliver me and my family from any habits, hang-ups, or hurts that the curse of iniquity has punished us with. By Your mercy, remove all guilt, condemnation, and shame from my life and the lives of my family. And now, Father, please begin to speak Your blessings into our lives, so that we may enjoy with You the blessings of the Kingdom of God in our lives.

If there be any area of my life that I need to repent for, Holy Spirit, please show me Your truth. I ask this in the holy name of Jesus Christ. Amen!

Jesus' internal bleeding has redeemed and broken internal weakness; the curse line is severed! Hallelujah!
Everything lost in the dominion covenant has been ransomed—returned to its original state—by the blood of the Lamb!

Chapter 5

Created to Manage

Genesis 3:17 (KJV): **And unto Adam he said, Because thou hast hearkened unto the voice of thy wife, and hast eaten of the tree, of which I commanded thee , saying , Thou shalt not eat of it:** *cursed is the ground for thy sake*； **in sorrow shalt thou eat of it all the days of thy life.** [Emphasis added.]

G OD is talking to Adam when He said, "Cursed is the ground because of you." You see, God didn't curse the Earth; Adam did. Adam had rulership and dominion over the Earth and all things in the Earth. Evidently, he had the power to resist anything but temptation, (bad joke). Because Adam had been placed by God "to rule and cultivate" the Earth, Satan had to go through Adam.

Do you remember what Jesus prayed to the Father in the Garden of Gethsemane? "Not My will, but Thine be done."

Why did Jesus pray that? So He could ransom what Adam said and did in the Garden of Eden. In Adam's disobedience to the Father, he ate of the Tree of the Knowledge of Good and Evil. In turn, a curse was born and with the curse came separation from God. Adam, who had once been privileged to walk in the cool of the evening in fellowship with God Himself—yes, an incredible relationship—was now separated from His presence because of sin. My friend, sin still separates us from God, so the faster we repent, the faster fellowship is restored.

God says to Adam in Genesis 3:19 (NKJV): **By the sweat of your brow you will eat your food until you return to the ground, since from it you were taken; for dust you are and to dust you will return.**

Notice that man moved from ruler to slave. Now hard labor and sweat became his destiny—both mankind and the Earth living under a curse! To understand what Adam lost, we must first look at what he used to have. God gave Adam wealth up front.

Genesis 2:9-12 (NKJV): **And the LORD God made all kinds of trees grow out of the ground—trees that were pleasing to the eye and good for food. In the middle of the garden were the tree of life and the tree of the knowledge of good and evil. A river watering the garden flowed from Eden; from there it was separated into four headwaters. The name of the first is the Pishon; it winds through the entire land of Havilah, where there is gold. The gold of that land is good; aromatic resin and onyx are also there.**

Let me point out the keys to wealth in this verse.

1. "All kinds of trees grow"—food provision; the agriculture industry.
2. "River [...] flowed from Eden"—water, irrigation, power. Water is a ten-billion-dollar-a-year industry in the United States.
3. Gold—the foundation of money.
4. Resin—oil.
5. Onyx—precious stones or jewels, diamonds. 95% of the diamond industry is owned by Jews. According to law professor Barak Richman, trade in gemstones also used to be a highly portable livelihood (unlike, for example, farming), for when the Jews were periodically expelled from their home cities in Europe during anti-Semitic purges—and Jews were frequently prohibited from owning land and joining crafts or merchants' guilds. The main thing is the Hebrew people understand that the wealth and resources of God are provided and available for them to cultivate by stewardship.

If you invest in any of these five areas and manage properly (stewardship), wealth will come to your hands.

Look at the first five words in Genesis 2:9 (NIV): **"And the LORD God made."** God provided the resources that, in turn, were Adam's wealth. Do you know why you were created? Take a moment to reflect. *You were created to manage the wealth provided.* Will you let me prove it?

Genesis 2:4–5 (CJB): **Here is the history of the heavens and the earth when they were**

created. On the day when ADONAI, God, made earth and heaven, there was as yet no wild bush on the earth, and no wild plant had as yet sprung up; for ADONAI, God, had not caused it to rain on the earth, and *there was no one to cultivate the ground*. [Emphasis added.]

Mankind was created to rule, manage, and cultivate

God hasn't changed. If there is no rulership, management, or cultivation, there is poverty. Today, many sit around to walk to the mailbox and collect a government check that others have paid for. Stop that! Now, don't misunderstand. If you've recently lost your job or are going through some hard times, I believe it is okay to get that check. But don't allow the check to make you lazy and slothful. God wants to use you to finance the kingdom. God has provided all the resources—gifts, talents, land, gold, silver, oil, precious jewels, etc. So what are you doing with God's resources?

Would you like to be God's manager here on Earth?

Your ability to manage determines whether or not you will be successful. What is management? To manage means to supervise, handle, or direct skillfully, to execute administrative or supervisory direction of the property and resources under your authority. Proper management requires planning, organization, development, and administration in order to reach the designated goal—that is, to succeed in accomplishing God's will for you here on earth.

But **God can only trust you with what you can**

properly manage. So I need to ask this question: Can you be trusted with more?

Psalm 115:16 (NIV): **The highest heavens belong to the LORD, but the earth he has given to man.**

God has given the Earth to man, and we have not taken our responsibility seriously. What this means is, you have legal rights to the Earth and its resources. Please allow me to reiterate: God's desire is to give the Kingdom of Heaven to the Earth! Didn't Jesus pray, "Thy Kingdom come. Thy will be done in earth as it is in Heaven" (Matthew 6:10, KJV)?

Jesus always prayed the will of the Father. We must understand that the Kingdom of Heaven is a Kingdom of *more than enough*, and it is God's perfect will for us to manage and be good stewards of His resources here on Earth. Your ability to manage determines, in every area of your life, how much you are trusted with.

My son and I have made many outstanding memories while hunting and fishing together. As God taught me "Principles of Kingdominion" through these activities, I have been privileged to teach the same to my son Joshua. One of those principles learned, is how to manage your emotions.

Buck Fever

When my son Joshua was nine years old, we had practiced very diligently at his shooting a 223 rifle for deer hunting. He was a natural and became a very good shot. However, there is a phenomenon that must folks know nothing about, called "buck fever." Every true deer hunter who has ever harvested a buck can tell you about it, but none can explain it. The only thing I can tell you is, you shake and tremble; you can't breathe; your heart pounds until it seems like it will jump out of your chest. If you have never experienced it, you really won't understand all the fuss. It is kind of like reading the Bible without the Holy Spirit; you just don't understand.

Nonetheless, I said all that to say. But even though Joshua was a great shot, I didn't know, if an attack of "buck fever" came, whether he would be able to hold steady and make the shot. Would he be able to manage his emotions? After all, he was only nine years old.

In Kingdominion, if with the power of the dominion covenant, you assign a deer to come to you, coming is all he is going to do, because the deer is not going to commit suicide for you. What I am trying to say is, if you sow your seed for a buck and release your faith to receive the buck, he's coming to where you are—but if you miss, it is your fault. Thus the importance of managing your emotions!

I have a very good friend named Rick Turner who has, for many years, allowed me to hunt on his family's ranch. This piece of property is a little taste of heaven to anyone who likes the outdoors. Thousands of acres of prime habitat calls to me every year when hunting season begins, so the year that Joshua was nine, I gave Rick a call and asked whether I could bring my son to shoot a deer. Rick said, "Yeah, I'd love to see him get one!"

All the way to the ranch, I went over the basics with Joshua, and once we arrived we prayed together, released our faith for a buck, and asked God to help us control our emotions. Rick told me which area of the ranch he wanted us to hunt, and I agreed and told him we'd be back in about thirty. Rick laughed and said, "Sure you will."

The area we were going to hunt was a grassy marsh. As Joshua and I arrived, I could see the back of a deer with his head down, eating, on the other side of the marsh. I asked Joshua what he saw.

With excitement in his voice, he answered, "Dad, that's my deer."

I warned him to calm down; "buck fever" had already showed up. I asked Joshua to be very quiet while we stalked to within range. Using the cover of trees and brush we crawled on our bellies to a small opening. There Joshua prepared for a prone 150-yard shot across the marsh. I had been filming his hunts since he was seven years old, so once again I had the video camera rolling. As Joshua looked through the scope of his rifle, the deer lifted its head to look around, and what do you suppose we saw? Of all things, imagine this: a buck. Joshua got very excited; he eagerly asked, "Can I take 'im? Can I, Dad?"

The deer was broadside, so I whispered to Joshua, "Take a couple deep breaths, hold steady, and place the crosshairs right on the top of his shoulder, and he will never take a step." I could hear Joshua breathe and noticed him settle as I zoomed in on the deer.

Boom! The buck dropped straight to the ground. I had myself an absolute fit, saying, "Boy, oh boy, what a shot! Great job, son! I'm so proud of you; that was awesome!"

Joshua was grinning from ear to ear, as if he had fully expected what had just happened. *Wow!* What a morning!

Joshua looked at me and said, "Dad, we made a good memory, didn't we?"

I said, "We sure did," and I hugged him.

Joshua and I were back at the barn just before thirty minutes were up. I remarked to Rick, "I told you so!"

Rick said to Joshua, "Boy, you are something else! I have friends who've been hunting for years, who come hunting and never get a deer—and you get one in thirty minutes!"

I fully believe that the main reason my son is a great man of faith and a great father and husband today is because of the Kingdominion lessons he learned on our hunting and fishing trips together. Over the years, Joshua and I have had many hunts like the one mentioned and all of them have taught us something new about the Kingdom of God. There were times we were not successful, but it was because we missed or didn't manage our strategy properly, not because we didn't take dominion and have opportunity. Good stewardship and management skills are a must if you want to be successful in every arena of life.

Psalm 115:14-16 (NIV): **May the LORD make you increase, both you and your children. May you be blessed by the LORD, the Maker of heaven and earth. The highest heavens belong to the LORD, but the earth he has given to man.**

According to this passage from Psalms, who should increase? Both you and your future generations, because of good management, will experience multiplication from the Kingdom of Heaven. As verse 15 says, "May the Lord make you increase, both you and your children." Please be warned: the Bible teaches that bad management brings loss. However, good management brings prosperity, rewarded with still more and that my friend is the blessing of the LORD.

Good management applies resources in the most beneficial way. For example, when you make a hundred dollars, you do not spend it carelessly—but neither do you hoard it. One is as bad as the other. If you spend it meaninglessly, you have wasted the seed for self-centered reasons. And if you hoard it, you have stopped giving (sowing), which is equally selfish and irresponsible and offends God, as He owns all your money anyway. So as good stewards, we pay ten dollars in tithe as God requires, and in return we have ninety dollars blessed by God Himself! Would you rather have one hundred dollars' worth of cursing, for not paying tithe (Malachi 3:8) or ninety dollars' worth of blessing?

True management skills must be disciplined, so if you are not disciplined and have been a careless steward in your past, please repent for bad stewardship and ask God for discipline, wisdom, and understanding.

> Luke 16:10–12 (NIV): **Whoever can be trusted with very little can also be trusted with much, and whoever is dishonest with very little will also be dishonest with much. So if you have not been trustworthy in handling worldly wealth, who will trust you with true riches? And if you have not been trustworthy with someone else's property, who will give you property of your own?** [Emphasis added.]

If you cannot be trusted with the seed (resources)

God has already given you to sow, how can you be trusted with more? How can you be trusted with the true riches of the Kingdom? Management, stewardship of the seed God ministers to you, is what qualifies you for increase, the multiplication of the Kingdom.

There are in scripture sixteen parables about money and all give examples of stewardship. We must be responsible managers of God's resources; to do otherwise not only affect our finances but also affects the answers to our prayers. Have you ever noticed that good stewards have their prayers answered, while bad stewards blame God for being a respecter of persons? Bad stewards may constantly question God, with statements such as, "Why are *they* being blessed when I've been a Christian longer than they have?" Bad managers are always asking for something new, such as a new job or increase in salary, when they haven't paid tithe or given offerings. They are robbing God—all because there is a new dress or a new set of golf clubs they have to have. And then they wonder why their prayers are not being answered.

Good management requires diligence and consistent efforts. Are you supposed to be at work on time? Of course you are. Concerning honoring your boss and being a good steward of his and your time, you can never be early if you leave late. Discipline, diligence, and consistent efforts are required, and God honors you being responsible, even if you do not get along with your boss. Conflicts between boss and employee, at times, are simply a test from God to see if you are qualified for the next level of management and the next level means increase. Thus, good management will determine your level of resources.

Proverbs 13:22 (NIV): **A good man leaves an inheritance for his children's children, but a sinner's wealth is stored up for the righteous.**

Have you noticed that many sinners are wealthy, while many Christians are poor? Friend, God doesn't love them more than He loves you. His justice is righteous and true, even with the wicked. God rewards proper management, regardless of who the manager is. I know unbelievers whose businesses prosper even in the times of this recession, because they pay tithe and manage properly. That's right, unbelievers paying tithe, because they know it works, and the blessing of God is on their businesses when they do. Good management is rewarded, because God has given the Earth to mankind and appointed us to manage His resources.

Did you think these principles were only for believers? Allow me to ask this question: if you are a parent, do you only love your children when they are good? No, you love all your children, all the time, as does God. Proverbs 13:22 tells us that a good manager will leave his future generations an inheritance that will be worth talking about. The children will be proud of their parents, as will the grandchildren their grandparents.

As good managers of the resources of God, we must economize. In other words, maximize the minimum, in order to get the most out of the least. We should never waste; Jesus taught us this principle when He fed fifteen to twenty thousand people (five thousand men—not counting women and children) from five loaves and two fish.

Mark 6:43–44 (NIV): **And the disciples picked up twelve basketfuls of broken pieces of bread and fish. The number of the men who had eaten was five thousand.**

Have you ever noticed that there are usually are more women and children at church than there are men? The gathering at which Jesus fed the multitude was probably no different—thus the higher estimates. And after all were fed and satisfied, what did the disciples do? They picked up all that was left over. When God multiplies, there is always more than enough, and we should always be good stewards of that more-than-enough, the excess—the leftovers, if you please!

For example, when we leave the house, as good managers we should reset the thermostat so we can save money on heating. We should also plan our trips to town, so as not to burn needless gas. Do not leave the water running or the outside door open. My mother used to say, "Son, you were not born in a barn; close the door!" If you use a piece of paper to print information that you no longer need, flip the paper over and print on the other side later. Proper management brings the blessings of the Lord!

CHAPTER 6

Management Produces Multiplication

The Hundred-Thousand-Dollar Deal

SOME years back, God spoke to me about investing in the real estate market of foreclosures and what I call "need-to-sell" properties. The Holy Spirit said to me that when He said "Pursue," I should go for it as it would be as if the deal was already done.

The provision of the Lord came to me via witty ideas (Proverbs 8:12) from the Holy Spirit that, in turn, would make sense to the owners or agents of properties, and I would be able to close the deal. God did the same thing for me that He did for those in the parable of the talents. He gave me deals to manage well, using no money of my own. It truly was a God thing, as I had never had any training in the real estate business, so I had to listen to His voice.

To illustrate, for many years I was an International Evangelist and when I stopped traveling all around the world, I had very little money of my own to invest due to everything going back into the ministry. Oh, how the Lord was leading me to trust Him! And trust Him I did. I heard of an opportunity about a house that was available and told the owners that I was interested. The Holy Spirit gave me an idea of how to make it work; I told the owners that I had no money to put down, but if they would let me tie up the property, I would pay them monthly installments and within a year pay them the balance of their asking price of one hundred thousand dollars. The favor of Kingdominion showed up, and we closed the deal.

My wife and I cleaned and painted the house, having a spiritual experience—repaint, repaint, and thin no more! (Excuse me for my bad jokes.) Then we bought all new furniture for the house on a credit card, thanks to my Beacon credit score of 787—established from very bad credit within a 6 month period. I then placed a "For Sale by Owner" sign at the property. The house was so beautiful that the third person who looked at it bought it for $143,000.00. Hallelujah! After paying the first owners, I then paid cash for my next deal, and away we went.

If the Kingdom of Heaven operates like this—and Jesus says that it does—then we can be sure that Jesus wants you to be blessed. The Kingdom gives you opportunity so that you can prove yourself worthy of more. The Kingdom of Heaven is Jesus, and Jesus is making the investment in you.

In the parable of talents, we see management skills. I am constantly hearing believers asking God for all kinds of materialistic things, such as a new car—when they haven't taken care of the one they have. When you haven't checked or changed the oil, rotated the tires to get more miles out of them, done annual tune-ups, kept it clean, washed, and waxed, etc., do you really think your demanding a new car is going to get you one? You have failed miserably at managing the resources you already have. Why would you think the Kingdom of Heaven will give you a new house when you won't invite anyone over to enjoy the one you have?

Jesus said, "to each according to his own ability." God gives according to your ability to manage. We need to learn to properly manage the resources God has already given so He will trust us with more.

In the parable of the Talents—Jesus says that this is what the Kingdom of Heaven is like.

> Matthew 25:15 (NKJV): **And to one he gave five talents, to another two, and to another one,** *to each according to his own ability.* [Emphasis added.]

The master in the Parable of the Talents gave to each of his servants according to his own ability. So one received five talents, which was equivalent to a hundred years' wages. Another received two talents—forty years' wages. And the third received one talent, twenty years' wages—or, some believe, a lifetime's worth of wages—because he hadn't yet developed any abilities but was still given a chance to prove himself. They were *given according to the servants' ability to manage.*

I have a question for you, how much of their own money did the servants use? None! Not one penny came out of their pockets. All three were given the seed to manage and cultivate.

Here is the conclusion of the parable, Matthew 25:16–30 (NIV):

> Then He who had received the five talents went and *traded with them, and made another*

five talents. And likewise *he who had received two gained two more* also. But *he who had received one went and dug in the ground, and hid his lord's money.* After a long time the lord of those servants came and settled accounts with them. So he who had received five talents came and brought five other talents, saying, "Lord, you delivered to me five talents; look, I have gained five more talents besides them." His lord said to him, *"Well done, good and faithful servant; you were faithful over a few things, I will make you ruler over many things. Enter into the joy of your lord."* He also who had received two talents came and said, "Lord, you delivered to me two talents; look, I have gained two more talents besides them." His lord said to him, *"Well done, good and faithful servant; you have been faithful over a few things, I will make you ruler over many things. Enter into the joy of your lord."* Then he who had received the one talent came and said, "Lord, I knew you to be a hard man, reaping where you have not sown, and gathering where you have not scattered seed. And *I was afraid, and went and hid your talent in the ground.* Look, there you have what is yours." But his lord answered and said to him, "You wicked and lazy servant, you knew that I reap where I have not sown, and gather where I have not scattered seed. So you ought to have deposited my money with the bankers, and at my coming I would have received back my own with interest. Therefore *take the talent from him, and give it to him who has ten talents For to everyone who has, more will be given, and he will have abundance*; but from him who does not have, even what he has will be taken away. And cast the unprofitable servant into the outer darkness. There will be weeping and gnashing of teeth."

[Emphasis added.]

Do you realize that the only time God says, "Well done, good and faithful servant" is when you have managed His resources properly? Not because you sang in the choir or taught the toddlers. It is not in the sweet by and by, when we all get to heaven, that He says, "Well done." No! He will say to you in this life: "Well done, good and faithful servant." That is, "Thanks for proper stewardship!"

Have you ever considered that the Kingdom of Heaven is like management skills? This is very important to God—so much so that He placed it in the Holy Scriptures for us to better understand that we must know how to manage His money and resources properly. Money is our bartering system, here on Earth. It represents wealth, power, influence, and favor; it is how the earth-cursed kingdom operates.

Why should we be good managers of the Lord's money? Because God has chosen people like you and me to finance the Kingdom of Heaven here on Earth! We must have money to operate in this earth-cursed system, and if we have it, there will be others who will follow and listen, because money brings influence.

How you handle God's money determines how much you are trusted with. Jesus is illustrating how the Kingdom of Heaven operates; in Matthew 25:21 the master says, "You, sir, get a promotion! You have managed the resources I have given you properly, so now I will trust you with more, much more! I will make you *ruler* over many things here in this life."

Increase comes, multiplication comes, because of your ability to manage and because God has determined that you are worthy of more. Then He says, **"Enter into the joy of your Lord!"** Promotion always brings joy—but remember, it is good management that causes joy to come into your life.

> Matthew 25:29 (NKJV): **"For to everyone who has, more will be given, and he will have abundance."**

That, my friend, is God's Bailout Program! Whether you receive more depends on your stewardship and if you are a good steward of the resources of God, no matter what the arena, more will be given and abundance will come.

Watch how it works:

1. God gives the seed (resources) for you to rule, manage, and cultivate.
2. God, in turn, blesses your efforts with a magnificent harvest.
3. After the harvest, God gives you more; you move into the realm of abundance.

Glory! It is time to start living in abundance!

I would be remiss if I did not mention that bad management also makes God very upset. Look again at the following verses:

> Matthew 25:26–28 (NKJV): **"You wicked and**

lazy servant, you knew that I reap where I have not sown, and gather where I have not scattered seed. So you ought to have deposited *my money* **with the bankers, and at my coming I would have received back my own with interest. Therefore** *take the talent from him, and give it to him who has ten talents.* [Emphasis added.]

It seems to me that Jesus wants us to realize that the one who was given five talents actually had no original investment of his own, only ability. Starting with zero monies, the Kingdom of Heaven shows up, and because of his good stewardship ability (management skills), the Kingdom invests in this man—how much? How much is a "talent" worth? A talent was the largest unit in Greek currency, ten thousand denarii. According to Matthew 20:2, the parable of the workers, a denarius represented a day's fair wages at the time. How much is your daily wage? Multiply your daily wage by ten thousand, and then you have a comparison to the value of a talent.

For example, if you earn thirty thousand dollars per year, and you work five days a week for fifty-two weeks, you will make approximately $115.00 per day. Thus, a talent in your case is worth ten thousand times $115.00: $1,150,000.00. Not too shabby! Look how much God wants to bless you!

But the lord in the parable gave the first servant not just one but five talents. Can you imagine if this was gold at the price of $1256.00 per ounce, in 2010? Wow! And most scholars believe a talent was in the neighborhood of one hundred pounds in actual weight. That is *pounds*, not ounces!

Many have mistakenly believe that the Lord of the servants (God) came to take back what had been given—in the case of the first servant, five talents plus the increase, a total of ten talents (approximately one thousand pounds of gold). But watch carefully as this story unfolds. The servants' master rewards good management by saying in Matthew 25:23 (NKJV) **"Well done, good and faithful servant; you have been faithful over a few things, I will make you ruler over many things. Enter into the joy of your lord."**

Well, that is indeed a good reward, becoming ruler over many things, wouldn't you agree? But that is not all the reward. When the lord scolds the wicked, lazy servant, watch carefully what he says:

Matthew 25:28 (NKJV): **"Therefore *take the talent from him, and give it to him who has ten talents.*"** [Emphasis added.]

The master does not take anything away from the good servants. He said, "Give the one talent to him who *has* ten. *Has* ten; let me say again, *has*—not *had*—ten! Nothing was taken away from the good servant; quite the opposite. Now this good steward is given the one talent that the wicked servant had, which raises his seed to eleven talents—representing millions of dollars. This, friend, is the true Bible doctrine of Proverbs 13:22 (NIV):

But a sinner's wealth is stored up for the righteous.

But you can forget about sitting on the couch, doing nothing, waiting for God to take wealth from sinners and give to you, the righteous. He will not do it. God looks at your potential; if you have no motivation or desire to rule, manage, and cultivate what God has already given, you certainly are not going to be more responsible with more. May I respectfully submit that when God takes from one, in this passage He proves to whom He will give what has been taken—the just steward, the one who properly rules, manages, and cultivates:

Matthew 25:29 (NKJV): **For to everyone who has, more will be given, and he will have abundance.** [Emphasis added.]

Did you see that? God says, **"to everyone who has."** *Has what?* you might ask. To everyone who has the ability to rule, manage, and cultivate; thus, more will be given, and Jesus promises that you will have abundance.

Eleven talents (a vast fortune, remember) a promotion, rulership over many things, and all the joy you can possibly have; what could ever be better? I'm glad you asked! It also means your children, grandchildren, and great-grandchildren will have no worries. The finances are in place; your position and blessings are sure. Hallelujah! You cannot beat this bailout plan, which is **"according to your own ability."**

This earth-cursed kingdom says we are in a recession. That means millions of jobs have been lost.

People are struggling to hang on to their homes and possessions. But I want to remind you that the money hasn't disappeared. All of God's resources are still on this planet. The gold has not left the planet; it is still here on Earth. Precious jewels, oil, water, land—none of them have gone anywhere. They are still here.

Do you realize that the rich do not talk about money? They talk about ideas. Why? Ideas are what bring wealth. People bound by poverty sit around dreaming of winning the lottery, or get involved in another get-rich-quick scheme, while the wealthy talk about ideas. I again ask the question, "What are you doing with God's resources?"

Let's quit sitting around, waiting for God to drop wealth out of the heavens. He will not do it! However, He will invest in you. Let's become motivated by faith and ask God for a dream, a plan for reaching a goal. God never gives a dream without giving the abilities (resources, etc.) to see it come to pass in your life. This is God's bailout program, the provision of the Kingdom!

If what you have done in the past is not working in the recession, change your thinking. I have had to change mine in order to keep from losing assets. Yes, I had assets that were providing income, but now because of the recession and hard times, those same assets have become liabilities. What is the difference between an asset and a liability? Assets put money in your pocket, while liabilities take money out of your pocket. Let me give you an example of changing my thinking and turning liabilities into assets.

I use three principles: **measure**, **manage**, and **multiply**

MEASURE

Luke 14:28 (NIV): **"Suppose one of you wants to build a tower. Will he not first sit down and estimate the cost to see if he has enough money to complete it?"**

The first thing we must do is count the cost!

MANAGE

Luke16:1-2 (NIV): **Jesus told his disciples: "There was a rich man whose manager was accused of wasting his possessions. So he called him in and asked him, 'What is this I hear about you? Give an account of your management, because you cannot be manager any longer.'**

If you do not manage properly, you will lose what you have!

MULTIPLY

Matthew 13:23 (KJV): **But he that received seed into the good ground is he that heareth the word, and understandeth it; which also beareth fruit, and bringeth forth, some an hundredfold, some sixty, some thirty.**

Psalm 115:14 (NKJV): **May the Lord give you increase more and more, you and your children.**

Deuteronomy1:11 (KJV): **The LORD God of**

your fathers make you a thousand times so many more as ye are, and bless you, as he hath promised you!

God wants you to enjoy and realize the multiplication of the Kingdom of Heaven in your life. Yes, it is His desire for you to increase.

GOD BAILED ME OUT AGAIN

Recently I needed to sell a rental property that I had bought to flip—that is, sell immediately for profit. When the recession hit, as you know, the bottom fell out of the real estate market, so selling investment property is tough. So, the Holy Spirit gave me the "witty idea" of selling the property with an "Agreement for Deed."

> Proverbs 8:12 (KJV): **I wisdom dwell with prudence, and find out knowledge of witty inventions.**

An "Agreement for Deed" also known as "Contract for Deed" is simply an agreement with the buyer that you the seller will owner finance the property sold and when the balance is paid in full, you will sign the deed over to the buyer. It is legal and works great because you have no upkeep or repairs. You see the buyers act as owners not renters. All expenses concerning property are the buyers responsibility. Here is an example of how an "Agreement for Deed" works:

Management Produces Multiplication

Owners Buying price	$50,000.00
Selling price	$75,000.00
Down payment	$5000.00
Buyers Mortgage	$70,000.00
Term	30 years
Interest	10%
Monthly payment	$614.30
Total interest	$151,148.04
Total cost to buyer principal and interest	$226,148.04

The potential in this example is over four and a half times the owners initial investment of $50,000.00.

Note: The interest rate is up to you!

Here is the important thing to see: with owner financing, you are making money on money you didn't have. In the example, you paid $50,000.00 for the property, but not only are you making 10% interest—or 11%, or 12%, or *whatever you decide*—on your initial investment of $50,000.00, you are also making interest on $20,000.00 you didn't have. Remember, the mortgage is $70,000.00. In addition, you have $5,000.00 down payment in your pocket that you didn't have before, and if the buyers were to default, you would keep the down payment and also take the property back and sell it again. I have one property I have sold three times. Sweet!

Buying Price = $50,000.00 Selling Price = $75,000.00 Projected profit = $25,000.00
Less down payment = $5,000.00
Income = $175.51 per month on $20,000.00 at 10% interest
Interest Income on $20,000,00 = $43,185.15
Total Income = $63,185.15 on $20,000.00 you didn't have!

Recommendation: As the owner, you should escrow taxes and insurance into the buyer's monthly payment.

Modern-day believers, by and large, have God "in a box." They read God's Word and go to church but walk in unbelief. It's like they assume that because the Word of God is old, God no longer does the things He did in biblical times.

But God has not changed. He is the same yesterday, today, and forever. So many people are living under a poverty mindset—absolutely convinced that they cannot manage God's money. Of course you can; God says you can, and He wants to sow into your life. You just have to stop being bound to an earth-cursed system of limitations. Instead, be an **"eleven-talent steward," who knows how to rule, manage, and cultivate.**

Be encouraged; try this stuff out. Take a chance and believe ridiculous blessings from the Kingdom of Heaven are available for you. The Government of God wants you to represent His authority and His power, and declare what He has said—then do what He says you can do!

Psalm 112 teaches how to speak blessing into your life. I recommend that you use the power of declaration and speak these scriptures into your life every day. You will notice that the declaration starts with praise. Praise is what changes the atmosphere of your environment, giving you the power and correct attitude to rule and take dominion.

> Psalm112:1–6 (NIV): **Praise the LORD. Blessed is the man who fears the LORD, who finds great delight in his commands. His children will be mighty in the land; the generation of the upright will be blessed. Wealth and riches are in his house, and his righteousness endures forever. Even in darkness light dawns for the upright, for the gracious and compassionate and righteous man. Good will come to him who is generous and lends freely, who conducts his affairs with justice. Surely he will never be shaken; a righteous man will be remembered forever.**

Declaration:

- I will praise the Lord!
- I will reverence the Lord and be blessed.
- I delight in the Lord's commands.
- My children will be mighty and highly favored.
- I will live an upright life and receive the blessing of the Lord.
- Wealth and riches are in my house.
- My righteousness will stand forever.

- The Lord's light will shine on me even in darkness.
- Things go well for me because I am generous and I lend freely.
- I am blessed because I conduct my affairs with fairness.
- Evil will not overcome me.
- My righteousness will be remembered forever.

CHAPTER 7

The Government of God

Isaiah 9:6-7 (KJV): **For unto us a child is born, unto us a son is given: and the government shall be upon his shoulder: and his name shall be called Wonderful, Counsellor, The mighty God, The everlasting Father, The Prince of Peace. Of the increase of his government and peace there shall be no end, upon the throne of David, and upon his kingdom, to order it, and to establish it with judgment and with justice from henceforth even for ever. The zeal of the LORD of hosts will perform this.**

IN verse 6 of chapter 9, Isaiah prophesies that the greatest gift of all is coming: "To *us* a child is born! To *us* a son is—" What? He is given. Given to whom? *Us!* Oh, what a gift, such a magnificent gift was given: a savior, Christ the Lord. Without sin, He became the perfect sacrifice for the redemption offered to everyone who would believe.

Then verse 6 says, **"And the government will be on His shoulders."**

Here is something we need to know and understand: the government on Christ's shoulders represents the Kingdom and all the Kingdom has. The Kingdom of Heaven on His shoulder shows the absolute authority and limitless power given to Him by God the Father. That is power without measure, and Isaiah says it's on His shoulders. This is a reference to magistrates having a key laid on their shoulders as a sign of their office.

> Isaiah 22:22 (KJV): **The key of the house of David I will lay on His shoulder; so He shall open, and no one shall shut; and He shall shut and no one shall open.**

> Revelation 3:7 (NIV): **To the angel of the church in Philadelphia write: These are the words of him who is holy and true, who holds the key of David. What he opens no one can shut, and what he shuts no one can open.**

God the Father states through Isaiah and John the Revelator that He would place the key, which represents the Government of Heaven, the Kingdom, on the shoulder of Messiah. Jesus, who has the key—the government—on His shoulders has the power to open any and all things (doors) and no one could shut. He also has the power to shut anything He desires to shut and no one could open. This represents supreme power and authority; there is no higher authority.

Have you ever prayed for doors to be opened or closed? I certainly have. I want to make sure this is clear. Do you need favor, a new job, new direction, new purpose? What God opens, no one can shut! Do you have loved ones influenced by Satan? What He closes, no one can open!

I've had parents of rebellious children come to me for prayer. We would pray that the door through which Satan had gained legal access should be closed by Jesus, the Government of God. Why pray in this fashion? Because, when Jesus shuts the door, there is no man, no spirit, and no power above or below, that can open it again.

Isaiah 9:6 goes on to say,

> **"He will be called Wonderful"**—In the Hebrew, this word "wonderful" means "a wonder," a marvel, something extraordinary; in this case, a wonder of God's acts of judgment and redemption.
>
> **"Counselor"**—Someone who advises, consults, gives purpose, devises, or plans.
>
> **"Mighty God"**—The mightiest of champions, the chief; there is no one above Him.
>
> **"Everlasting Father"**—The head or founder of a household.
> **"Prince"**—Ruler of rulers.
>
> **"... of Peace"**—The completeness of God; God's safety, soundness in body, welfare, health; prosperity with God, especially when in covenant relationship.
>
> Verse 7 says, **"of the increase of His government and peace there will be no end."**

There will be no end, there will be no end, hope your understanding what the word of God declared, there will be no end to the Government of God. Did you know there are some Christians who are actually afraid that Islam will take over our country and one day rule the world? They are quick to tell you there are already ten to twelve million Muslims in America. Statistics say that the Muslim population is growing at a rate of 2.7 percent, which is faster than the birth rate of humans in the entire world, currently at 2.3 percent. But repeat these words to yourself: "I'm not worried, because God said that there will be no end to His Government or to the increase of His Kingdom." All other religions are temporary!

Hey, that is better than the Energizer Bunny! The Kingdom of God keeps growing and growing and growing!

Isaiah 9:7b (KJV): **... upon the throne of David, and upon his kingdom, to order it, and to establish it with judgment and with justice from henceforth even for ever. The zeal of the LORD of hosts will perform this.**

Christ will reign on David's throne. Oh, saints, remember that, in the Davidic Covenant, God told David, **"Your throne will be established forever"** (2 Samuel 7:16). This is the very thing Isaiah's prophecy is talking about. Jesus is from the lineage of David, and He is the Lion of the Tribe of Judah. He is King of Kings and Lord of Lords, and He is the fulfillment of both the Davidic Covenant and Isaiah's prophecy.

Then verse 7 states, **"Establishing and upholding it [the Kingdom] with justice."**

To understand how the Government of God operates, you must understand the word "justice." The Hebrew word is **Ts@daqah**. Its definition is "righteousness," "right standing," or simply "rights"!

Isaiah is prophesying what Jesus would accomplish. Isaiah says, "A Messiah is coming, to give every believer their rights! Unto us a child is born, unto us a son is given, and the Government of God will be on His shoulders!" (Isaiah 9:6)

Jesus had the strength needed to take the sins of the world on Himself and overcome them because He has Kingdominion. He *is* the Kingdom. He *is* the Government. He *is* God!

AS A BELIEVER YOU ARE A MEMBER OF THE HOUSEHOLD OF GOD

Ephesians 2:19 (NKJV): **Now, therefore, you are no longer strangers and foreigners, but fellow citizens with the saints and members of the household of God.**

Not everyone is a member of the household of God. God's love paid an awesome price, the death of His Son, for everyone to have the opportunity to be a member of His family. But God wants us to have a choice, and not everyone chooses to be a member of the household of God. Isn't that sad? The price has been paid in full by Jesus Christ, for all mankind to have membership in the family of God. Yet many turn their back on access to the Kingdom of Heaven and all that it represents.

Ephesians 2:19 tells believers that we are no longer strangers or foreigners but members of the household of God. This has become one of my favorite verses in all of scripture. Why? Because it proves that I have rights in the Kingdom of Heaven. It says that the believer is *no longer a stranger.* The Greek word used here is *xenos*, which means without the knowledge of, without a share in. In Bible times, Aliens did not have rights and were illegal.

Then it says, **"Nor are we foreigners."** The Greek word used here is *par'oy kos*, which means "One who has no right of citizenship." But this verse says that we, as believers, have become members of the household of God. You are a member, you are kindred, you belong, you have rights of intimacy, and you are related by blood. You have rights to inherit. You are God's child.

I'm doing my best to try to explain who you are in Christ. Answers to prayers do not come because of emotion, high praise, or fasting. No, you get your answers because you are a member of the household of God. You have rights to what the Kingdom has to give.

Isaiah 9:7b says, **"He [the Messiah] will reign on David's throne and over His Kingdom, establishing and upholding it with justice and righteousness from that time on and forever."**

In a court, justice is upheld, to get you, the citizen, what is rightfully yours! As a citizen, you have governmental rights. If you are a law-abiding citizen, the laws of the government have given you rights—as long as you abide by the law!

Again, to make sure you believe you are a citizen, look at what God's Word says about you:

Hebrews 2:11 (NLT): **So now Jesus and the ones he makes holy have the same Father. That is why Jesus is not ashamed to call them his brothers and sisters.**

We have the same Father. We are brothers and sisters of Jesus. Do you know your rights?

You have rights to everything available to the household of God. There is no sickness, no disease, no infirmity, and no lack. You do not have to be subject to financial recession, famine, or depression. The household of God offers favor, authority, power, abundance, love, unity, dominion, and much, much more. Doesn't the Word say, **"But seek ye first the Kingdom of God and all these things will be given added to you?"** (Matthew 6:33 [KJV])

Do you remember the story of blind Bartemaeus, in chapter 10 of Mark? Bartemaeus, a blind man, sat by the road begging, but when he heard that Jesus was passing by, he began to cry out—because he believed the prophecy of Isaiah 9:6-7—"Jesus, thou son of David, have mercy on me!" When Jesus heard what Bartemaeus was saying, I think He probably said to Himself, "Someone knows who I am; someone understands that I have the Government of the Kingdom on my shoulder."

> And they came to Jericho: and as he went out of Jericho with his disciples and a great number of people, blind Bartimaeus, the son of Timaeus, sat by the highway side begging. And when he

heard that it was Jesus of Nazareth, he began to cry out, and say, Jesus, thou Son of David, have mercy on me. And many charged him that he should hold his peace: but he cried the more a great deal, Thou Son of David, have mercy on me. And Jesus stood still, and commanded him to be called. And they call the blind man, saying unto him, Be of good comfort, rise; he calleth thee. And he, casting away his garment, rose, and came to Jesus. And Jesus answered and said unto him, What wilt thou that I should do unto thee? The blind man said unto him, Lord, that I might receive my sight. And Jesus said unto him, Go thy way; thy faith hath made thee whole. And immediately he received his sight, and followed Jesus in the way. (Mark 10:46–52 [KJV])

Bartemaeus was immediately healed because he understood and had faith in the Government of God. Notice that his healing was immediate and not a long, drawn-out process; God wants to accelerate your Bailout.

And Jesus said to Bartemaeus, "Go thy way. Thy faith hath made thee whole"—not just healed, but made whole. Oh my goodness, I will take wholeness over healing any day, because wholeness means that everything is made new.

Let's look again at these very important points of Isaiah 9:

Verses 6,7… **and the government shall be upon His shoulders…He shall reign on David's throne and over his kingdom.**

Also, Isaiah 22:22 (KJV): **And the key of the house of David will I lay upon His shoulder.**

When you recognize that you are a member of the household of God and know your rights, Jesus, the Government of God, will give you your rights. Yes, He will see to it that you get what you have rights to.

The last phrase of Isaiah 9:7 states, **"The zeal of the Lord Almighty will accomplish this."** Nothing can stand in God's way where your rights are concerned. Every right you have, and every right you declare, when declared, the zeal of the Lord will give to you. He will accomplish all that needs to be accomplished.

Have you ever thought that God had zeal? This word "zeal" in the Hebrew is *qin'ah*, meaning ardor, jealousy, jealous disposition (as of a husband), sexual passion, ardor of zeal (of religious zeal) as of men for God, of men for the house of God, of God for his people, or of men against adversaries. God is crazy about you! He is passionate to see you blessed and to see you live in His abundance. His zeal will accomplish all that is needed for you to gain your Kingdom Rights. When you recognize who you are in Christ, you have the opportunity to live as a family member in the household of God, enjoying all the benefits promised.

Establishing and Upholding with Justice

Isaiah 9:7b: **establishing and upholding it with justice and righteousness from that time on and forever.**

As we learned earlier in this chapter the word

"justice" translated from Hebrew means *rights!* Remember that it is justice that compels the honorable judge to get you, the citizen, what is rightfully yours—all because you have *rights!*

Do you realize as a citizen of the Kingdom of Heaven, you have legal rights and access to the Government of God and all the Kingdom of Heaven has, every day you live? In Matthew chapter 6 Jesus prayed the model prayer and said, "Thy Kingdom come," and we have mistaken this to be referring to the second coming of Christ. He was saying you have the right to ask that the authority and power of the Kingdom of Heaven be in operation in your life daily. Yes, you have the rights for the will of God in your life today. "Thy will be done"; where? "In earth as it is in heaven."

I like to pray the Lord's Model Prayer this way:

Matthew 6:9 (KJV): **"My Father, which art in heaven, hallowed be Thy name."**

Here I spend time praising the Lord for who He is in my life, as with "My Father in Heaven, how wonderful and majestic is Your name. Your name is above all names. You are wonderful, counselor, the Mighty God, the Lover of all that I am. I give You all Glory and praise!"

10: **"Thy Kingdom come. Thy will be done ..."**

"Kingdom of God, come into my life today. Come into my life, Kingdom rulership, authority, and power of the Kingdom, which as a child of the household of

God, I have rights to. May the will of God be done in my life today, in my family, my church, and my business."

"... in earth as it is in Heaven."

This phrase is often assumed to mean the whole Earth. I beg to differ. You and I are earthen vessels, made from the Earth by the hands of God. So I pray, "Let the will of God be done in this physical body You have given me, in this earthen vessel, as it is in the Kingdom of Heaven."

11: "Give us this day, our daily bread."

Notice that this prayer is now dealing with the physical need of your earthen vessel. Thus, I pray, "I release the economy of the Kingdom, the provision of the Kingdom of God, into my life today. Release into my life and the lives of my family all that is needed socially, financially, and physically." Remember that this is a daily prayer.

12: "And forgive us our debts, as we forgive our debtors."

Here is the spiritual application. Repentance always deals with the spirit man, and our repentance is very important to God. He said in verses 14 and 15 of this same chapter 6 of Matthew, **"For if ye forgive men their trespasses, your heavenly Father will also forgive you: but if ye forgive not men their trespasses, neither will your Father forgive your trespasses."**

Take this very seriously, as it is the only way to get your prayer answered. I pray, "Forgive my sins, O Lord, as I fully and freely forgive others for their sins against me. I understand, according to Your Word, that I must forgive in order to be forgiven. Please give me Your abilities to forgive so that I can not only forgive those who have sinned against me but also forget what they have done."

13a: "And lead us not into temptation, but deliver us from evil."

This deals through prayer with the soul of man. Your soul is your mind (your thoughts), emotions, and will. God has given you the gift of choice, the right to freely make decisions. Jesus shows us how to defeat the enemy daily, by teaching us to subdue our thoughts. The thought process is where the evil one tempts. It is where we choose to turn away from or pursue temptations.

When I pray this portion of the prayer, I declare, "Father, I purpose and choose to follow You and You alone, and I ask You to deliver me from the evil one. Deliver and protect me from his temptations, trials, and traps."

13b: "For Thine is the Kingdom and the power and the glory, for ever. Amen."

Did you notice that the Lord's Model Prayer not only begins but also ends with praise? I believe that praise should make up two-thirds of our prayer time, because praise brings the habitation of the Lord (Psalm 22:3). When God inhabits your praise and you experience

His manifested presence in your life, what more could you possibly want?

In the Lord's Prayer, Jesus demonstrates how we should live, as members of the household of God. You have the right for the Kingdom of God to come into your life daily. You have the right for the will of God, His healing, deliverance, peace, joy, security, blessing, and prosperity, to show up in your life today. You have the right for the provision of the Kingdom to manifest. You have the right to be delivered from the evil one.

Let's read the Constitution of the Government of God, His Word, to find out exactly what our rights are.

> You have the right to pray, "Lord, bless and enlarge my territory" (1 Chronicles 4:10).

> You have the right that the devourer is to be rebuked by God Himself, because you are a tither (Malachi 3:11).

> You have the right to lay hands on the sick and watch them recover (Mark 16:18).

> You have the right to cast out demons and tell them they can never return (Mark 9:25).

> You have the right to declare that no weapon that comes against you shall prosper (Isaiah 54:17).

> You have the right to take authority over the entire enemy (Luke 10:19).

You have the right to have supernatural power (Acts 1:8).

This is victorious living. This is what Jesus said was a more abundant life. This is Kingdominion.

Now let us quickly review what we have learned in this chapter. "The government shall be upon His [Jesus'] shoulders." This means the Messiah is the absolute, who has all authority and power in the Kingdom of Heaven. If there is a Kingdom, there must be a King. Isaiah declares, "Unto us a child is born, unto us a son is given." This child, this son, is none other than the King of Kings, Yeshua, the Christ. Hallelujah!

We have also learned that Messiah will reign on David's throne and over his Kingdom. This means that His ruling authority will increase, and there will be no limitation to the wholeness He will give. He will rule from the historic throne of David over the Kingdom of Heaven. He will establish and uphold the Kingdom with *justice*.

We have learned that His justice means rights, and as citizens of the household of God, we have the right to declare and receive what God has said and promised us.

CHAPTER 8

God's Security Program

THE DECLARATION OF INDEPENDENCE

"WE hold these truths to be self-evident, that all men are created equal, that they are endowed by their Creator with certain unalienable rights, that among these are life, liberty and the pursuit of happiness."

What are "unalienable rights"? The absolute rights of individuals may be resolved into the right of **personal security**, the right of personal liberty, and the right to acquire and enjoy property or possessions. These rights are declared to be natural rights, inherent and yes, unalienable.

If you do not know that in the Government of God you have the right to **personal security**, you can't possess it. If you do not know that God's Government declares you can have liberty, you will continue to be bound by habits, addictions, and hang-ups. And furthermore, in the Government, you have the right to live in peace and happiness—but if you do not claim these you will walk around grumbling and complaining.

THE ARMY OF THE GOVERNMENT OF GOD

At this point, I need to address the subject of the army of God. It is my desire to show you, through the Word, that we should not be defeated in our war against sin and demonic powers.

We have been told by preachers and denominations that as children of God, we are in the Army of the Lord. What the Word states is that we are to be *as* soldiers, to have the mentality of a soldier—but the Word never says we *are* soldiers. Rather, it states that we are family of the household of God. Would you rather be a soldier in the army of the Lord or be defended by the army of God?

The Apostle Paul tells us to put on the whole armor of God, which is for protection against Satan's attack against us personally in the earth-cursed realm. This is what we term "spiritual warfare," and, yes, it is very real in the spirit realm.

> Ephesians 6:13-17 (NIV): **Therefore put on the full armor of God, so that when the day of evil comes, you may be able to stand your ground, and after you have done everything, to stand. Stand firm then, with the belt of truth buckled around your waist, with the breastplate of righteousness in place, and with your feet fitted with the readiness that comes from the gospel of peace. In addition to all this, take up the shield of faith, with which you can extinguish all the flaming arrows of the evil one. Take the helmet of**

salvation and the sword of the Spirit, which is the word of God.

Notice that this is God's armor, which means that when you wear it, you will be supernaturally protected. Also, you see there is only one offensive weapon, and that is the "Sword of the Spirit." That, my friend, is all we need. Let's take a look at this armor.

1. **Belt of Truth.** Our reproductive system is protected with truth. Jesus said "I am the way, the truth, and the life" (John 14:6).
2. **Breastplate of Righteousness.** Our vital organs are protected by righteousness. The Word teaches that Jesus was manifested to take away our sin, and in exchange He has given us His righteousness (1 John 3:5–7).
3. **Gospel of Peace.** Here we see that our feet are shod with the gospel of peace. This is foundational, as footwork is the most important thing in combat. John 14:27 (KJV) says, "Peace I leave with you, my peace I give unto you: not as the world giveth, give I unto you."
4. **Shield of Faith.** A shield is for your defense; it protects you from the attack of the enemy. In spiritual war, the Shield of Faith protects you from the flaming arrows of temptation, accusation, and intimidation, which are sent by Satan, The Bible says, "Jesus [is] the author and finisher of our faith" (Hebrews 12:2).
5. **Helmet of Salvation.** The Word of God says of Jesus, in Acts 4:12 (KJV): "Neither is there salvation in any other: for there is none other name under heaven given among men,

whereby we must be saved." The name of salvation is Jesus!

6. **Sword of the Spirit the Word of God.** The word of God declares in Hebrews 4:12 (KJV): "For the word of God is quick, and powerful, and sharper than any twoedged sword." Also, John 1:1 tells us that Jesus is the Word.

When you put on each piece of armor, you are actually putting on Jesus. He is our defender. And when you take up the Sword of the Spirit, you can defeat any devil simply with your declaration of what Jesus has already said about your situation. Jesus should always be between you and the enemy's attack!

As a citizen, you have the right to defend yourself, your property and possessions, and your family. But the fact that you have rights to defend yourself as a citizen doesn't mean you are a soldier in the Army of the government of the United States of America, or by faith the Army of God. What it really means is that you have rights!

> The Apostle Paul states, in Ephesians 6:10–12 (NIV): **Finally, be strong** *in the Lord* **and in** *his mighty power.* **Put on the** *full armor of God* **so that you can take your** *stand against the devil's schemes.* **For** *our struggle is not against flesh and blood***, but against the rulers, against the authorities, against the powers of this dark world and against the spiritual forces of evil in the heavenly realms.**

Who is Paul talking to? He is speaking to believers,

to members of the household of God. What he is explaining is that there is a power that is far above every other power, and this awesome power defeats every assailant. This power has a name, and it is Jesus!

We have been discussing the Keys to the Kingdom of Heaven, but please allow me to simplify things: *Jesus is the Key!* It is Jesus who has dominion, authority, power, and might; He is Ruler; He is the defender of our faith. He is our Redeemer and Deliverer, He is our Healer, and He is *King of Kings and Lord of Lords!*

HOW WE MAKE WAR

> Revelation 19:6-7 (CJB): **Then I heard what sounded like the roar of a huge crowd, like the sound of rushing waters, like loud peals of thunder, saying, "Halleluyah! ADONAI, *God of heaven's armies*, has begun his reign! *Let us rejoice and be glad! Let us give him the glory!*"** [Emphasis added.]

Here we get a glimpse of how we are to make war: "Adonai, God of heaven's armies, has begun his reign! Let *us* rejoice and be glad! Let *us* give him the glory!" The extent of our warring is with honor, praise, and glory!

> Revelation 19:11-15 (NIV): **I saw heaven standing open and there before me was a white horse, whose rider is called Faithful and True. With justice *he judges and makes war*. His eyes are like blazing fire, and on his head are many crowns. He has a name written on him that no one knows but he**

himself. He is dressed in a robe dipped in blood, and his name is the Word of God. *The armies of heaven were following him,* **riding on white horses and dressed in fine linen, white and clean.** *Out of his mouth comes a sharp sword with which to strike down the nations.* **"He will rule them with an iron scepter."** [Emphasis added.]

This passage states that Jesus judges and makes war. Verse 14 says that the armies of—where? The armies of Heaven follow Him. The Greek then explains that He then makes war and strikes down the nations with a "two-mouthed" sword—meaning that it speaks blessing to the faithful and curses evil. It cuts away everything that is not needed, and when withdrawn it brings healing. Then the Word declares that *Jesus rules* with an iron scepter—meaning He has supreme power and authority. His authority is over every king and kingdom. Hallelujah!

Did you know the only way to remove a king is to be backed by a King with greater authority? His name is *Jesus!*

So many Christian believers are fighting and warring in their own power, and they become burned-out and distraught, weary from what they call "spiritual warfare."

But Jesus said in Matthew 11:28–30 (NIV): **"Come to me, all you who are weary and burdened, and I will give you rest.** *Take my yoke upon you* **and learn from me, for I am gentle and humble in heart,** <u>**and you will**</u>

find rest for your souls. For my yoke is easy and my burden is light." [Emphasis added.]

Do you get that? Jesus is saying, "Give me the burden; give me the fight. I have already defeated every foe and taken dominion over every kingdom the enemy has. Don't struggle with this burden; give it to me, because my yoke is *easy*, and my burden is *light!*"

When you take Jesus' yoke, you become a carrier of Jesus Himself, His presence, His power, His anointing and authority. And when this takes place, you are no longer warring; rather Jesus is fighting for you. And the good news is Jesus wins every time!

2 Corinthians 10:3-6 (CJB): **For although we do live in the world,** *we do not wage war in a worldly way;* **because** *the weapons we use* **to wage war are not worldly. On the contrary** *they have God's power for demolishing strongholds.* **We demolish arguments and every arrogance that raises itself up against the knowledge of God; we take every thought captive and make it obey the Messiah. And when you have become completely obedient, then we will be ready to punish every act of disobedience.** [Emphasis added.]

The weapons of spiritual warfare are God's weapons, not ours. They are not worldly ways—guns, knives, martial arts, the military, or any other human thing. These weapons have God's anointing on them to absolutely destroy every stronghold that has plagued your life. His abilities are all-powerful.

What we do is demolish every proud argument that Satan brings, simply by obedience to Christ, and then punish every act of disobedience with our confession.

THEN WHO IS THE ARMY OF THE LORD?

Jesus said in John 18:36 (KJV): **My kingdom is not of this world: if my kingdom were of this world, then would my servants fight, that I should not be delivered to the Jews: but now is my kingdom not from hence.**

Jesus was saying to Pilate, "Neither my Kingdom nor my servants are of this world." The word in the Greek that is translated as "servants" literally means "soldiers of the King." Jesus said He could pray to His Father and call twelve legions of angels. A legion at that time was 6,100 foot soldiers and 726 horsemen.

Matthew 26:53 (KJV): **Thinkest thou that I cannot now pray to my Father, and he shall presently give me more than twelve legions of angels?**

2 Kings 19:35 (KJV): **The angel of the Lord killed 185,000 in one night.**

This is just one soldier—or should I say, angel? This soldier is one bad dude. Now can you see why we are not qualified to be in God's army? These soldiers, the angels, are not just supernaturally strong but also supernaturally fast. The word of God gives evidence that they can move at the speed of light—that is, 186,000 miles per second. That is the ability to travel around the earth 7 ½ times in one second. Any one soldier who can travel at that speed and kill 185,000 in one night, I'm very glad I'm on his side!

> Psalm 78:49 (KJV): **God dispatched against them a band of destroying angels.**

> Luke 2:13 (KJV) speaks of **"a multitude of heavenly host."**

> Joel 2:11 (KJV): **And the Lord shall utter His voice before His army.**

This army is not us, but the heavenly host—the army of God.

> Revelation 19:19 (KJV): **Then I saw the beast and the kings of the earth and their armies gathered together to make war against the rider on the horse and his army.**

> Joshua 5:14 (KJV): **"I am the Captain of the Army of God."**

In the passage from the Book of Joshua, Jesus is telling Joshua that He is the Captain of the Host of the Lord. Joshua fell on his face in worship, and because he worshipped, victory came to him and to the Israelites.

We may have been taught that we are fighting when we pray or when we fast. No, that is disciplining ourselves to be able to focus on God instead of on our problems. My brother Troy preaches a great message, entitled "Where the Focus Goes, the Power Flows." We must learn to be able to focus properly, and prayer and fasting are two of the tools we use to bring about such a discipline.

The Book of Daniel gives a perfect example of our warfare:

> Daniel 10:12-13 (NLT): **Then he said, "Don't be afraid, Daniel. Since the first day you began to pray for understanding and to humble yourself before your God, your request has been heard in heaven. I have come in answer to your prayer.** *But for twenty-one days the spirit prince of the kingdom of Persia blocked my way. Then Michael, one of the archangels, came to help me,* **and I left him there with the spirit prince of the kingdom of Persia.** [Emphasis added.]

Daniel prayed, and God heard and sent an angel to take him the answer to his prayer. Then something spectacular happened. The Bible says that the prince of the kingdom of Persia fought against the angel, the messenger of the Lord.

On the twenty-first day afterward, Daniel was still praying the same prayer. Daniel wasn't fighting; he was praying. Although sometimes the religious crowd makes praying a battle, we must remember that prayer should always begin and end with praise—and praise is a celebration, not a battle.

Please don't misunderstand; I know there are times we contend and stand in the gap in order to bear one another's burdens—but we also must remember that **Jesus has already defeated our enemies, so our battle is already won. Jesus said it is *finished!***

The reason the believers have so many battles is because we really do not believe it is finished. Yes, we live in an earth-cursed system, and yes, there are trials and tribulations; yes, we must stand our ground and let Satan know we resist his attacks, as he is most assuredly trying to destroy our witness, character, and lives. But the question is, are we going to take our hands off and rest in the finished work of the cross? *It is finished!* What this means is, if we trust God, no matter what is thrown at us, no matter what we go through, we will have victory in Jesus.

In Daniel's case we see the true picture of spiritual warfare. The angel of God was doing the fighting. Where was the fighting taking place, you might ask? In the heavens—or, as we would say, in the second heaven. You see, the prince of the kingdom of Persia was an evil, dark spirit, a principality, and the angel of God was from the Kingdom of Light. So when the two met, there was a battle. Twenty-one days they fought—but remember, delays are not denials. Sometimes your answer is delayed because of a battle in the heavens. This is the reason we need to know and understand these things.

God has given us the Keys to the Kingdom, which are the power to bind and loose; we have rights to bind here on earth, and then God binds in the heavens. If ever your prayer is delayed, bind the hindering forces of Satan in the name of Jesus. Then God, if He needs to, will—as He did with Daniel—send Michael, the warring angel, to bind the principality that is keeping your answer from you, which in turn will enable you to obtain your request. That is exactly what happened with Daniel, and God loves us so much that He placed this example in the Bible so we could understand the nature of spiritual warfare.

> Psalm 103:20-22 (NLT): **Praise the LORD, you angels of his, you mighty creatures who carry out his plans, listening for each of his commands. Yes, praise the LORD, *you armies of angels* who serve him and do his will! Praise the LORD, everything he has created, everywhere in his kingdom. As for me—I, too, will praise the LORD.** [Emphasis added.]

Praise is what gets the job done. Praise Him, praise Him, praise Him! Here again, the passage from Psalms teaches us that the Army of God, the angels, serve to do the will of God and the Kingdom.

> Hebrews 1:14 (NLT): **But angels are only servants. They are spirits sent from God to care for those who will receive salvation.**

Can you see it? The angels are servants to whom? They are servants to members of the household of God. They are sent to minister to and protect us. Glory to God! They will act as our bodyguards, if we will release them to do so.

In the Kingdom of God, citizens do not fight. With us, as it was with Daniel, the army of God—the angels—fight to defend and protect us, the citizens of the Kingdom. Now, if you are just bent on fighting, have at it—but I'd rather be resting. I would rather live in *shalom*, the very peace of God.

IN THE NATURAL REALM

In the United States, as citizens, we have the right to call 911 when we need help. When we do, firefighters, police, or paramedics—people who work for the government—come in a hurry, with lights flashing and sirens sounding. Why? Because of the rights of the citizens.

Let me ask, does the United States have an army? Not only do we have an army, but our soldiers are enlisted in the Marines, Air Force, Navy, and Coast Guard as well. If war breaks out, who is going to battle? The government and all the soldiers who represent this government's military. Are citizens going to fight? No! The Army, Navy, Air Force, and Marines are going to fight, because they are protecting the citizens. They are fighting for the rights of our citizenship. All you have to do is sit at home and watch the battle on television, because you are not in the Army; you are a citizen.

God says in His Word that He will send His angel before you (Genesis 24:7, Exodus 23:20). What do you think that means? His angel is here to clear the way, to protect, to fight your battles for you. God told Jehoshaphat in 2 Chronicles 20:15, **"Don't be afraid or discouraged because of this vast army. For the battle is not yours, but God's."**

Jehoshaphat, the king of Judah, had three nations coming against him. He called the people of Judah to pray and fast. Then God showed up and said, "Don't be afraid."

If you study this passage, you will see that God gives instructions to send out Judah. The Hebrew meaning of the name "Judah" is "praise." So Jehoshaphat sent out ten thousand praisers before the enemy, without a weapon in their hands, and when they began to shout, sing, and dance in their praise, confusion came to the enemy. And the armies of the three enemy nations became confused and killed one another!

Remember, God said to the people of Judah, "You will not fight in this battle, for the battle is the Lord's." Many thousands died that day. Three complete armies of the enemy lay slain, because praise confuses the enemy. When praise goes up, God shows up.

All Jehoshaphat and Judah did was praise God and then pick up the spoils. There was so much plunder (things of value) that it took them three days to gather it all. Hallelujah!

Psalm 149 is one of my favorite chapters in the Bible, and verse 6 states, **"Let the high praise of God be in your mouth."** Then God says in verse 8 of this chapter, that because high praise has gone up, **"I will bind the kings with chains and their nobles with fetters of iron."**

One day in study, the Lord showed me this was what we term "spiritual warfare." He said to me that when we praise Him, He will show up and bind the enemy's kings and nobles—which are principalities, powers of the air, rulers of the darkness, and spirits of wickedness (Ephesians 6:12). God said, "Your praise releases Me to bind as if with chains and iron shackles, to bring you victory!"

I hope you are seeing this. It is this high praise spoken about in Psalm 149 that releases God and the hosts of Heaven to bind our enemies. Do you remember what Jesus said about the Keys to the Kingdom of Heaven?

Matthew 16:19 (KJV): **And I will give unto thee the keys of the kingdom of heaven: and whatsoever thou shalt bind on earth shall be bound in heaven: and whatsoever thou shalt loose on earth shall be loosed in heaven.**

Our battles are not with flesh and blood (Ephesians 6:12) but with the demonic powers of the kingdom of darkness. And exactly like the example of Daniel, when we begin to pray to and praise the Most Holy God, we are, in effect, binding here on earth—and then God binds (defeats) our enemies in the heavenlies on our behalf, and gives us the victory.

Religion teaches that we have to fight and struggle from day to day. But the Government of God states that although there will be various trials and tribulations, we as citizens have the right to have the *shalom* (peace) of God and live in His abundance and rest while God's army defends our rights. I don't know about you, but I'd rather trust God to do my fighting—because He has never lost a battle.

CHAPTER 9

Ambassadors of Christ

DO you know anyone who has questioned God? When there is limitation, we have a tendency to ask God *why*, and some even blame God for their limitations. May I tell you, we are the ones who limit, not God!

In the natural world, there is a process for sowing and reaping, just as there is in the supernatural realm. Because we are living in harvest time where the things of the Kingdom of God are concerned, God speeds up the harvest time dramatically for the believer, in reaping the blessings of the Kingdom. But in order to reap a harvest, you must first sow the seed.

However, there are also the blessings of the inheritance, which is provision given from what others have previously sown and reaped. If you are to receive an inheritance in the kingdom of this world, there is a process that you must go through, because the government is involved, due to someone leaving a will, in which they specify who should receive what of their possessions and financial assets. The Kingdom of Heaven works basically the same way; blessings from the Kingdom of Heaven are given because you are in the Father's will.

2 Peter 1:3 (NKJV) says, **"the divine power [power of the Kingdom] has given to us all things that pertain to life and godliness."**

If it has been given, we have legal access to it! As we learned in Chapter 2, there is a process that we must use in the Kingdom of God, of binding and loosing, and we must understand how it works. Then all you have to do is release your faith to believe, and you shall have (Mark 11:24). These blessings are yours by inheritance, because as a believer you have become a member of God's family!

What are some of these things that pertain to life and godliness? The power of the kingdom of God has given us breath, health, provision, favor, influence, authority, power, etc. If you do not have these in your life, I have good news for you: they are available!

Have you ever noticed that when the Bible talks about you, the believer, it doesn't refer to you as sorry, lazy, good-for-nothing, or trifling? It calls you king, priest, ruler, ambassador. You need to know who you are and what you should be doing; don't you agree? In this chapter, I want to talk about your opportunity to be an ambassador for Christ.

By the sacrifice of Jesus, you have a right to be an ambassador, an agent of the Government of God. If you do not bind, then who will? If you do not loose, it will not be loosed. To see the Kingdom operate in your life, you must turn the key, because as a believer, you have already been granted access! You have been given the Keys to the Kingdom.

Jesus has, through His sacrifice, given you the right to be His ambassador.

2 Corinthians 5:20 (NKJV): **Now then, we are ambassadors for Christ, as though God were pleading through us: We implore you on Christ's behalf, be reconciled to God.**

Do you realize what this means? Ambassadors are formal diplomatic agents who are appointed to represent the dignity of their sovereign (or head of state) and are **entitled to personal access to their sovereign.**

All believers have the right to be ambassadors, but because most do not realize their rightful position, they continue to be bound by an earth-cursed kingdom instead of being liberated with the authority and power of the Kingdom of Heaven.

WHAT AMBASSADORS DO

Ambassadors believe in and abide by their government's Constitution and represent their sovereign, going to other nations on his behalf. The Constitution of the Government of God is His word, the Bible.

The Apostle Paul was an ambassador of Christ. Philemon 1:9b: **"I am Paul the ambassador of Christ Jesus."**

You should be recognized as an ambassador. What are you waiting for?

BENEFITS OF AMBASSADORS

Every ambassador has access to an embassy. An embassy is not just owned by the ambassador's government; it is legally considered the sovereign territory of that government. Embassies contain the offices of the ambassador and the ambassador's staff. The staff members are diplomatic representatives who serve under the ambassador.

I liken embassies to the Cities of Refuge that the Hebrews had access to in the Old Testament of the Bible. Whenever Old Testament Jews, the Hebrews, were in trouble, they could always find safety and protection in the City of Refuge. No one could touch, do harm, imprison, or seek vengeance against anyone who had sought safety in the City of Refuge. An embassy works the same way. It, too, is a place of protection and safety from any avenger in the earth-cursed government.

WHY IS ALL THIS INFORMATION IMPORTANT TO ME?

Simply because, if you do not understand how the Government of God operates, you will not be able to release the power of the Government in your daily life.

As an ambassador, we represent the head of state of our Government, which is Jesus!

The head of state is the individual or collective office that serves as the chief representative of a nation. In nation-states such as the USA, the head of state is the official leader of the nation or government—in our case, the president.

DIPLOMATIC IMMUNITY

One of the perks of being an ambassador is having diplomatic immunity. Diplomatic immunity ensures that diplomats are given safe passage through other countries and are considered not susceptible to lawsuit or prosecution under their host government's laws. Diplomatic immunity protects diplomats working outside their home country. Immunity is freedom from punishment, harm, or loss.

This is huge! When you learn to release this kind of power and authority into your life, you will indeed realize that the Prince of the Power of the Air (Satan; Ephesians 2:2) does not have legal rights to attack, punish, persecute, prosecute or imprison you, because you are an ambassador of Christ and of the Government of God, which legally gives you diplomatic immunity. In the spirit realm you are "above the law." The prince of this world, and his principalities, powers, rulers of the darkness of this age, and spiritual hosts of wickedness in the heavenly places (Ephesians 6:12 [NKJV]), do not have legal rights to you, the ambassador of Christ. Remember, Earth is not the source of our government. Our government is the Kingdom of Heaven.

THE MESSAGE OF THE GOVERNMENT OF GOD

> Mark 1:14–15 (NKJV): **Now after John was put in prison, Jesus came to Galilee, preaching the gospel of the kingdom of God, and saying, "The time is fulfilled, and the kingdom of God is at hand. Repent, and believe in the gospel."**

The kingdom of God arrived with the presence of the King. What did Jesus preach? He preached the gospel of the Kingdom, which is "the Good News." Jesus was saying, "I've come to ransom all that has been lost due to the sin curse."

Matthew 4:23 (NIV): **Jesus went throughout Galilee, teaching in their synagogues, preaching the good news of the kingdom, and healing every disease and sickness among the people.**

Matthew 9:35 (NIV): **Jesus went through all the towns and villages, teaching in their synagogues, preaching the good news of the kingdom and healing every disease and sickness.**

Matthew 11:5 (NIV): **The blind receive sight, the lame walk, those who have leprosy are cured, the deaf hear, the dead are raised, and the good news is preached to the poor.**

It is very evident from these verses that, when you declare what your government says—as Jesus did by preaching "the Good News of the kingdom"—then the power to heal every sickness and disease is available. When the Kingdominion of God shows up, the blind see, the lame walk, the deaf hear, and the dead are raised. Hallelujah! These are simply some of the perks that are available to you as an ambassador of Christ. But what I want you to notice is the last phrase of Matthew 11: 5: **"the good news is preached to the poor."**

What would be good news to the poor? Good news would be that you do not have to be poor anymore; you can be blessed, and you can live in prosperity! Hallelujah! Now that is good news!

JOB OF AN AMBASSADOR

Being an ambassador for Christ is not something hard and stressful. Why? Because you do not have to give an opinion, nor do you have to back anything up. You do not have to have a solution or all the answers. You simply repeat what your government has already said. As an ambassador, you have no right to represent yourself. You represent the Government of God. Thus, you should never give your personal opinion.

CONCERNING YOUR OPINION

I have a very dear friend who died and had an out-of-body experience. She tells the story of actually going to Heaven and hearing God say that she could not stay but must return and tell all who would listen "to be of no opinion."

Of course there is much more to the story, but the message she brought back from the portals of Heaven should make us all repent. We live in a day and time when everyone has an opinion. Just stop and ask someone what they think. It doesn't matter what you ask; just ask, and you will hear an opinion. Especially in the "Bride of Christ," there have been so many church splits, over nothing more than an opinion.

And to think that God, the "Ancient of Days," sent my friend back to this earth-cursed kingdom to tell us, "Be of no opinion." When what Jesus thinks and says becomes more important that what we think or say, then and only then do we have the right to be His ambassadors.

So when the earth-cursed kingdom asks you a question, as an ambassador, say, "My government says ..." For example:

- When someone wants someone else's wife or husband, your response would be, "My government says, 'Thou shalt not covet your neighbor's spouse.'"
- To the question of idolatry, reply, "My government says, 'You shall have no other gods before God Jehovah.'"
- To the question of rebellion, "My government says, 'Rebellion is as the sin of witchcraft.'"
- To the question of disobedient children, "My government says, 'Children, obey your parents in the Lord, for this is right ... Honor your father and your mother.'"
- To the question of cursing, "My government says, 'Do not take the name of the Lord in vain.'"
- To the question of extra-marital sex, "My government says, 'Do not commit adultery.'"
- To the question of murder, "My government says, 'Do not kill.'"
- To the question of theft, "My government says, 'Do not steal.'"
- To the question of lying, "My government says, 'Do not bear false witness against your neighbor.'"
- To the question of sickness or disease, "My government says, 'By the stripes of Jesus you were healed.'"
- To the question of being demonized "My government says, 'I am given power over all devils.'"

- To the question of past hurts, "My government says, 'Jesus came to heal the brokenhearted.'"
- To the question of barrenness, "My government says, 'The fruit of your womb will be blessed.'"
- To the question of increase, "My government says, 'Everything you set your hands to will prosper.'"
- To the question of favor, "My government says, 'I will be made the head and not the tail.'"

When my Government speaks, *the question is settled.*
Psalm 119:89 (KJV): **For ever, O LORD, thy word is settled in heaven.**

AS AN AMBASSADOR, THE KINGDOM FLOWS OUT OF YOUR HEART AND WORDS

Remember Mark 11:24 (KJV): **"What things soever ye desire, when ye pray, believe that ye receive them, and ye shall have them."**

In order to receive what you pray for, there must be a spiritual alignment between your "heart's desiring and mouth's declaring." The key to having your desire align with God's desire for you is found in the Word of God:

Psalm 37:4 (KJV): **"Delight yourself in the Lord and He will give you the desires of your heart."**

Many people use this scripture to try to get what they want, when, in truth, it is all about giving. "Delight yourself in the Lord" means that we should praise God without any ulterior motive. You come to God *giving* Him praise. You praise Him because you love Him, because you want to enjoy His presence, because of who He is in your life. You are not praising Him in order to get something for yourself but to give Him glory and adoration for being the God of your life.

If it is hard for you to praise Him, you have not established a relationship with Him. He should be as your best friend, the one whom you can tell anything and everything to. What is so hard about that? Have you forgotten, He already knows your secrets, because He sees and knows everything about you?

What happens when you praise Him in this fashion? He, in turn, comes to where you are and inhabits—or sets up habitation with—you.

Psalm 8:2 (NIV): **From the lips of children and infants you have ordained praise because of your enemies, to silence the foe and the avenger.**

The word "ordained" in this scripture means "to set, to build or establish a throne." When you praise God like a child—uninhibited, not caring who's watching, free, and celebrating who He is in your life—then God inhabits your praise and builds a throne in your heart, where He comes and sits down together with you. Praise the Lord!

The rest of Psalm 37:4 then states, **"And He will give you the desires of your heart."**

This does not mean He is going to give you just

any old thing you desire. *No!* What it means is, you will not want anything outside the perfect will of God for your life, because you were praising Him with no ulterior motive. When we do this, God places His desire for your life into your heart, **giving to you all things that pertain to life and godliness.** He gives you the mysteries of God, the hidden treasures of God, the purpose and destiny that He desires for you. *Wow!*

What do you think He wants for you? He wants you to have the very best!

CHAPTER 10

The Blessing of the Lord Brings Wealth

Proverbs 10:22 (NKJV): **The blessing of the Lord makes one rich, And He adds no sorrow with it.**

HAVE you ever seen an ambassador riding in an old, rusted-out automobile? Of course not. They are always in the finest, with flags flying and a full military escort.

Do you understand that last phrase, "a full military escort"? Ambassadors do not fight, but they do have complete and total protection from the government they represent. In the Kingdom of Heaven, this military is called the Heavenly Host, which is the Army of God. Yes, the Army of the Lord.

As mentioned earlier, the Bible declares in Ephesians 2:19 that the saints are members of the household of God. Citizens do not fight but have rights to be protected by the government. However, it is the angelic hosts of the Kingdom of Heaven who protect you and give you a full military escort as an ambassador of Christ. Doesn't that get your motor going?

THE BLESSING OF THE LORD

When, the Word—that is, Jesus—talks about the blessing of the Lord in Proverbs 10:22, He is not talking about material things. Rather, He is talking about the covenant of God, the dominion covenant of Genesis 1:26. In Genesis 9:1-3, the covenant is reestablished through Noah, and then again in the Abrahamic covenant (Genesis, chapters 15 and 17). And we are the seed of Abraham. His covenant is filled with the blessings of prosperity, health, wholeness, favor, and success.

TIMOTHY'S KINGDOMINION BOW HUNT

For many years, I spent my free time bow hunting and became very good at it. Some professionals said I was one of the best in the world. In developing these skills, I had an advantage: I'd learned early on that if I would honor God, He would honor me. Whether I was preaching, singing, working, fishing or hunting, it didn't matter. Kingdominion showed up wherever I was, because it was in me. Remember, it is in you!

One day, my nephew, Timothy, who was in his midteens at the time, asked me to take him bow hunting. His desire was to harvest a deer with his bow. At that time, he had never harvested one with either gun or bow. Since it was bow season, we set out for the woods.

I decided to film the hunt. Timothy and I then prayed to take dominion over the beast of the field, the deer, and set out. With video camera in hand, I taught him how to follow me as we stalked—that's right, stalked! To stalk means to pursue quarry or prey stealthily (I told you I am good at this.)

This particular morning, we—the Holy Spirit and

I—had gotten Timothy within range, about 20 yards away, on three different deer, and he had not taken a shot. Each time, he complained that the angle was wrong, or a bush or a limb was in the way. I explained that dominion provides the deer, but you must shoot. Then, losing some patience, I told Timothy that the next time I said "Shoot!" and he didn't, I was going to kick his behind up between his ears, and he'd look funny with two sets of cheeks!

In a few minutes, we were on a spike buck, with camera rolling. Oh, you should have been there; Timothy made a perfect shot. As we watched the deer fall, Tim must have jumped four feet in the air, and it seemed that when he kicked his feet, he went that much higher! I filmed as Timothy jumped, danced, and ran around, shouting "Thank you, Jesus! Thank you, Jesus! Thank you, Jesus!" Kingdominion began teaching a teenager how to rule and dominate his environment.

Now let me ask you, what are the chances of two people with camera in hand slipping and stalking within twenty yards of four different deer in one morning? Let me answer this way: you go give it a try!

Oh, friend, when you release your faith to believe that what you set out to do will be accomplished, let me tell you, all things are possible. We are not bound by an earth-cursed system of *can't*; indeed, you *can*, with the authority God has given you!

When I was a boy, my parents taught me to pray about everything. At six years of age, I remember very clearly praying to do well as I stood in left field playing little league baseball. While praying, I heard the crowd screaming my name, so I stopped praying and opened my eyes to see the baseball rolling past me. So I learned early on to do as Jesus instructed us: *watch* and pray! (Ha!) The point is, even as a child, I was praying about everything that was important to me.

My parents enabled and encouraged me to hunt and fish. Thus, I developed a passion for the outdoors. It seems I learned how to release the power of Kingdominion in my life while hunting or fishing, as the Holy Spirit was constantly telling me to take dominion. So I began to say things like, "I take dominion over the fish of the sea," or, "I take dominion over the deer in the woods." God began to bless my declarations with successes and prosperity that, to the natural mind, just didn't make sense. I knew that I would have to be careful who I shared these experiences with, because most people—even believers—thought I was lying. But I continued to release my faith for ridiculous stuff. Have you ever believed God for the ridiculous?

CATCHIN' A WILD DEER

Let me give you an example. My son Joshua, my brother Troy, his sons Timothy and Trent, and I, along with my sister Alethea's son Jeremy, were riding through the woods of Florida, hunting wild hogs, when a deer crossed in front of us. I said, "I can catch him if you want!" Trent started laughing. Joshua believed I could do just about anything, and Troy has done some pretty ridiculous things himself, so he just smiled. Jeremy and Timothy, following in another truck, had no idea what was happening.

Trent said, "Uncle Lem, you're good, but that's a wild deer!"

I said, "Challenge! Stop the truck!"

You see, Kingdominion allows you to dominate your

The Blessing of the Lord Brings Wealth

environment. Didn't God say in Genesis 1:26 that we have dominion over the beasts of the field? I eased out of the truck and told the others to stay inside and leave the motor running. Deer are very nervous by nature, so if I'd slammed the door of the truck or cut the motor off, the deer would probably have spooked and run off.

Now, this deer was wild and in the woods, which, of course, is his proper environment. We had only gotten a glimpse before he was hidden behind brush again, traveling through the woods. I made a trek through the woods to head him off. When I got into position, I peeked around some palmettos and saw him coming toward me. When he got within about five or six feet, I stepped out from behind my cover and raised both my hands straight up to Heaven. I don't know why I lifted my hands; I guess I'm so used to raising my hands in praise to Jesus that it was simply the natural thing to do.

When I did this, the deer lay down. I bent down and picked him up in my arms. He never kicked. He was not nervous or afraid and did not try to get away. For a white-tailed deer, that was an absolute miracle! He stayed calmly in my arms as I carried him back to the truck.

I wish you could have seen everyone's faces when I walked to the truck holding a wild deer in my arms. I just sat down in the truck, and said, "Your turn!"

It was hilarious! After everyone petted the deer I let it go. He did not flee in fear; *no!* He calmly walked back into the woods. We do not dominate with fear tactics like our adversary, the devil; we dominate because of God-given Kingdom authority and power.

The *shalom* (peace) of God in my life changed the environment that day, causing all the natural fears the deer would normally have to disappear. Oh, it's good to be an ambassador!

GOD WANTS TO TEACH YOU ABOUT HIS KINGDOM

> Prov. 10:22 (NKJV): **The blessing of the Lord makes one rich, and He adds no sorrow with it.**

Are you tired of failing? The blessing of the Lord, His covenant, says that we have dominion. When you realize that you really have this kind of authority in your life, you will walk in the blessing of the Lord—yes, the favor and success of the Lord. God wants you to be successful, and the most wonderful thing is, He'll use the things that we love to do, to teach us about His Kingdom. For me, He used hunting and fishing.

Let me ask you a question. Do you think that it will be hard for me to believe that God can heal someone, or believe that God can help us become debt-free, after I've caught a wild deer with my bare hands? Absolutely not! Faith increases when you've seen the impossible. That's the reason I've seen so many miracles in my life and in the lives of others. God is awesome!

By the way, catching the deer that day wasn't a fluke; I've caught several with my bare hands, and many times showed them the power of "Kingdominion" just for fun. What an awesome covenant we have!

THE OFFICE OF AMBASSADOR

There is another scripture that we must understand in order to walk in the office of ambassador:

Psalm 8:4–9 (KJV): **What is man that You are mindful of him, And the son of man that You visit him? For You have made him a little lower than the angels, And You have crowned him with glory and honor. You have made him to have dominion** *over the works of Your hands*; **You have** <u>put all things under</u> *his feet*, **All sheep and oxen—Even the beasts of the field, The birds of the air, And the fish of the sea That pass through the paths of the seas. O Lord, our Lord, How excellent is Your name in all the earth!** [Emphasis added.]

When God created Adam, He created him to rule. Neither Adam nor you were created to be subordinate. Again, "King-dominion" means "ruler domination."

IT'S TME TO TAKE DOMINION

Genesis1:26 (NKJV): **Then God said, "Let us make man in our image, according to Our likeness;** *let them have dominion* **over the fish of the sea, over the birds of the air, and over the cattle, over all the earth and over every creeping that that creeps on the earth."** [Emphasis added.]

In this passage, we see that Adam was given power over all the Earth—but not just Adam. Verse 26 says, "Let *them* have dominion"—Adam and everyone to come, which, of course, includes you. Now we know and understand that Adam lost his authority to rule because he ate of the Tree of Knowledge of Good and

Evil. God personally told him, "Don't eat of this tree." Because of Adam's disobedience the Earth was cursed. But may I remind you, Jesus redeemed the curse by His blood and ransomed—bought back—everything that had been lost; so we now have Kingdominion authority once again!

SINCE THE SIN CURSE

God's desire has been to "restore His Kingdom of Heaven on earth." Everyone wants power and success; it's in our DNA. God placed it in each of us because He wants you to rule as a king. Have you ever noticed that when children play, they play to win? When my brothers John and Troy and I were children, we often played "King of the Mountain." We all wanted to be king. It is in us to rule and dominate.

The desire to rule was even more pronounced in my interactions with my sister Alethea. When we were growing up, she often tried to boss me around—and I her, as she was two and a half years younger than me. But how many of you know, that didn't work! I've had to repent for the ways that I mistreated my sister. What I couldn't see before was that the desire God placed in my sister, to rule and dominate, is a gift and a calling in her life that has made her a powerful intercessor and psalmist. And let me just add, if you come against me in any way, you will have my sister to fight as well. Praise God for His benevolent blessings of the love of family!

Now don't misunderstand; I'm not talking about domination out of pride and ego or a controlling spirit. No! Everything about the kingdom of God is wrapped in the love of God and His compassion. However, I am talking about dominating your environment and circumstance. Doesn't the Word say, **"When the enemy comes in like a flood, the Spirit of the Lord will lift up a standard against him"** (Isaiah 59:19 NKJV)? What is this standard? The standard is the Kingdom of God!

The enemy doesn't have a chance, because he, too, is under our feet. Now for those of you who have to have New Testament proof that the dominion covenant is for today, let's look at Hebrews 2:7–8 (NKJV):

> **You have made him [man] a little lower than the angels; You have crowned him with glory and honor, And** *set him over the works of Your hands. You have put all things in subjection under his feet.* [Emphasis added.]

When was this accomplished? The moment Jesus said, *"It is finished"* (John 19:30). That was when the "dominion covenant" was restored to everyone who will believe. Power and authority has been given to us by Jesus, to rule and dominate—power over all the works of the Creator's hands; in other words, all things created. That includes Satan and his dinky demons. Praise the Lord!

Allow me to show you some differences between the earth-cursed kingdom and the Kingdom of Heaven, or Kingdomionion:

Earth-cursed kingdom
gives no power over your environment.
gives tolerance to endure pain and suffering
makes you accept your circumstances
hates change

Kingdominion
rules and dominates in the love of God
gives power and authority to heal the sick and raise the dead
gives power and authority cast out devils
embraces the impossible
loves change

AS AMBASSADOR, YOU HAVE DOMINION POWER

Let's review Hebrews 2:7 (KJV): **Thou madest him** [man] **a little lower than the angels; thou crownedst him with glory and honour, and didst set him over the works of thy hands:** [Emphasis added.]

What does a crown represent? The power and authority of the government. Glory represents the manifested power and presence of the self-existent eternal God! I hope you're getting this, because, beloved, this is good stuff!

No wonder all things are possible. In Mark 9:23, Jesus said, **"If you can believe, all things are possible to him who believes."**

As an ambassador, God has crowned you with the power and authority of the government, and then if that is not enough, God's glory, His manifested power and presence, comes to where you are. He never sends you by yourself; remember, He, the Kingdom, is in you!

As air is to the atmosphere of Earth, so glory is to the atmosphere of the Kingdom of Heaven. Isaiah 60:1 (KJV) says, **"Arise, shine; for thy light is come, and the glory of the Lord is risen upon thee!"**

Arise—get up out of your complacency! Arise—stand up with boldness! Shine, for your light is come; like the morning sun breaking over the horizon, its glorious rays illuminate the earth! Shine, shine, shine! You are the light of the world; a city set on a hill cannot be hid (Matthew 5:14). Come on, saints, it is time to allow the light of the Kingdom of God to shine through us so brightly that the earth-cursed kingdom will see our good works and glorify our Father who is in Heaven!

Hebrews 2:7 continues by saying, **"And set him [man] over the works of Your hand."** [Emphasis added.]

This word "set" means "to place one over a thing, in charge of it; to appoint one to be administrator of an office." What office? The office of an ambassador. Oh, I'm getting blessed as I write this—blessed enough to go catch a deer!

As I write, just two short weeks ago, one of my parishioners had an open vision in church on Sunday morning as I preached concerning Ambassadors and the Kingdom of Heaven. In the vision, the roof of the sanctuary rolled back, and she was able to look directly into the heavens. She saw a great crown descending from Heaven. When it reached our sanctuary, it completely covered the church and began to spin.

What do you think the Holy Spirit was saying? I believe the crown in the vision represents the Kingship of Jesus and the Government of God. His power and authority, have come to this house, this fellowship, and God wants us, the believers, to take our rightful position as ambassadors. If we will simply believe and say,

"Yes," we, as ambassadors, will indeed be crowned with glory and honor!

The spinning crown represented the joy of the Lord—or should I say, the Government of God, celebrating the fact that our fellowship of believers is entering into the authority and power given by the Kingdom. God wants this to happen in your life; He desires you to be an ambassador for Christ! He wants you have Kingdomion, ruler domination!

CHAPTER 11

Time to Rule and Dominate

> John 6:63 (NIV): **The Spirit gives life; the flesh counts for nothing. The words I have spoken to you are spirit and they are life.**

THIS statement is pregnant with mystery, life, and power! Remember, Jesus decided to lay divinity aside and became one hundred percent human. In so doing, He became the Lamb, slain from the foundation of the world. He lived thirty years of His life in human frailty. He had no supernatural power, *until* ...

The Holy Spirit empowered Jesus when the Spirit descended upon Him! At that moment the Kingdom of Heaven invaded earth.

> John 5:19-21(NIV): **Jesus gave them this answer: "I tell you the truth, the Son can do nothing by himself;** *he can do only what he sees his Father doing, because whatever the Father does the Son also does.* **For the Father loves the Son and shows him all he does. Yes, to your amazement he will show him even greater things than these. For just as the Father raises the dead and gives them**

life, even so the Son gives life to whom he is pleased to give it."** [Emphasis added.]

What I want you to see from verse 19 is; *the Son can do nothing by Himself.* At first, Jesus had absolutely no capabilities for the supernatural, as He chose to live outside the divine nature in human flesh, exactly like you and me—100% human, and thus limited.

However, when the Holy Spirit descended upon Jesus after His baptism (John 1:32), He became empowered for the supernatural. Hallelujah! Empowered to heal the sick, cure disease, cast out demons, cleanse lepers, raise the dead, give sight to the blind, unstop deaf ears, make lame legs walk and run, heal the brokenhearted, multiply loaves and fish to feed many thousands, speak to angry winds and command them to be still, defy gravity, and walk on water ... Are you getting the picture?

Now remember, it is Jesus talking when He says, **"the Son can do nothing by himself; he can do only what he sees his Father doing."**

Jesus only did what He saw the Father do! Every believer has same human limitation in the earth-cursed kingdom, but every believer also has access to the same supernatural power from the Kingdom of Heaven.

THE SECRET TO KINGDOMINION

What is the secret of Kingdominion? In order to operate in the supernatural, you must be able to **"see what the Father is doing"** and **"hear what the Father is saying."**

John 14:24 (KJV): **Jesus said: "the word which ye hear is not mine, but the Father's which sent me"**

We must be able to hear what the Father is saying in order to do the miracles Jesus did. Is it possible for people like you and me to see and hear what our Father God is doing and saying?

USE WHAT IS IN YOU

Matthew 16:1-3 (KJV): **The Pharisees also with the Sadducees came, and tempting desired him that he would shew them a sign from heaven. He answered and said unto them, When it is evening, ye say , It will be fair weather: for the sky is red. And in the morning, It will be foul weather to day: for the sky is red and lowring.** *O ye_hypocrites, ye can discern the face of the sky; but can ye not discern the signs of the times?* [Emphasis added.]

The Pharisees were a group of around six thousand Jews who prided themselves on their outward works. The Pharisees were always trying to impress others, with their fasting, prayers, and almsgiving. They had an attitude of, "Look how holy and righteous I am! See what I have done!" The Saducees were a religious party who denied the following doctrines:

- Resurrection of the body
- Immortality of the soul
- Existence of spirits and angels

- Divine predestination

(No wonder they were "Sad, you see"!)

Both religious sects operated only based on what they had learned and experienced, operating in natural gifts but not spiritual gifts. They applied no *faith!* In Matthew 16:1-3, Jesus was saying, "It's in you to operate in the spiritual [supernatural], but you are hypocrites for not using what God has placed within you."

I wonder what would happen in most churches if Jesus showed up next Sunday in bodily form. What would He say to believers? Would He call us hypocrites for not using the gifts He has placed within us?

May each and every reader of this book realize that it is within us to discern the times; the faith is within us to believe for the impossible (Romans 12:3); it is within us to rule and dominate our environments. Yet the question begs for an honest answer: are we using what has been placed within?

WHAT, EXACTLY, IS WITHIN US?

Luke 17:21 (NIV): **the Kingdom of God is within you.**

If we are not careful, we will become like the Pharisees, trying to get into Heaven with our good works. Thus, we develop a religious spirit—constantly trying to "good works" our way into heaven—instead of developing a relationship with Jesus who will assure us of the blessings of the Lord now and eternally.

At this point, I must remind you that God is not

lost; you do not have to seek for Him. He is available to you whenever you call His name. He's never too busy to talk to you.

NEGATIVE THINKING

Have you ever noticed that most modern day Christians emphasize not hearing the voice of the Lord? By example: "God is not talking, and if He is, I can't hear Him!" Saying things such as, "I've never seen a vision, an angel, or a miracle! God must be a respecter of people; otherwise, why does He talk to Brother [or Sister] Know-It-All and not to me?"

Have you ever considered that God wants you to see what He is doing and also hear what He is saying? It is called communication—and that, my friend, is what develops a relationship.

CONCERNING COMMUNICATION

The one who desires to communicate has the responsibility to make sure he is heard. Does God desire a relationship with you? Of course He does, because He desires a family, and he wants you to be one of His children. How, then, do you build a relationship with your Heavenly Father?

Communication is the most important facet when building or establishing a relationship. And the thing you must realize is God wants to communicate—to talk—with you. God wants you to hear what He has to say. The problem is not with God; it is with us. Have you ever been at a college football game, where there are thousands of people? The band is playing, the cheerleaders are cheering, people are screaming and yelling because your favorite player just scored a touchdown—and now your best friend is trying to tell you something. You find that with all the distractions, it is nearly impossible to hear—yet what do you do? You lean closer, giving your full attention to what is being said, and you shout, *"Talk louder! I can't hear you!"*

If you have many distractions in life and find it difficult to hear what the Father says, ask Him to talk louder. In His desire to communicate, He will make sure you can hear.

WHY WE NEED TO HEAR

> John 6:63 (NIV): **My words are *spirit* and *life*.** [Emphasis added.]

Jesus is telling us that, when His words are spoken, the Holy Spirit is released and escorts His words to an open heart. Why is this important?

> Roman 14:17 (KJV): **For the Kingdom of God is not meat and drink; but righteousness, and peace, and joy in the Holy Ghost.**

The Kingdom of God is not of or from the natural, earth-cursed realm. Jesus is saying, the Kingdom of God does not operate by earth-cursed methods, or by human beings' so-called wisdom. It operates in the supernatural realm of **righteousness, peace, and joy**—*in the Holy Spirit!*

The Kingdom of God is *righteousness*. This word in the Greek text means "the condition acceptable to God"; that is, right standing or justice. You receive justice in a courtroom because of your rights, and as a citizen of the Government of God, you have rights to all that the Government of God has to offer.

The Kingdom of God is *peace*. The word "peace," in Greek, means a state of national tranquility, exemption from the rage and havoc of war. It implies peace between individuals—harmony, concord, security, safety, prosperity, felicity ... because peace and harmony make and keep things safe and prosperous. It also speaks of the Messiah's peace, the way that leads to peace (salvation) of the believer and the tranquil state of a soul assured of its salvation through Christ. This causes us to fear nothing so we become content with earthly life.

The Kingdom of God is *joy*. Nehemiah 8:10 explains, "the Joy of the Lord is our strength"! Thus, the Kingdom of God is joy, gladness, and the strength of God Almighty Himself.

But wait! This declaration is not over! For then the Word of God in Romans 14:17 adds four very important words: ***"in the Holy Spirit."*** All these attributes of the Kingdom of God are wrapped in the Holy Spirit; thus, you cannot have the supernatural rights of justice, peace, or joy, without the Holy Spirit.

THE REALM OF THE SPIRIT IS THE REALM OF THE KINGDOM OF HEAVEN

You can't have the glory—the manifested power and presence of God—without the Holy Spirit. The Holy Spirit demonstrates and manifests the Kingship of Jesus. And when Jesus the King is manifested, the Kingdom is manifested. You see, the Kingdom of Heaven is the realm of Jesus' dominion.

Whenever you speak what the Father speaks, the Holy Spirit is released—and because He is released, the Kingdom of God is manifested. This is proven by what the people said in Luke 4:36 (NLT): **"What authority and power this man's words possess! Even evil spirits obey him and flee at his command!"**

The same power and authority Jesus operated in, He has given to us, the believers.

WHAT HAS HE GIVEN US? THE SAME THINGS THE FATHER GAVE HIM!

> Matthew 11:27 (NLT): **My Father has given me authority over everything.**

> John 10:10 (KJV): **The thief cometh not, but for to steal, and to kill, and to destroy: I am come that they might have life, and that they might have it more abundantly.**

Jesus wants to give you everything He has, so that you can have life abundantly.

Some years back I used to hold revival services in Franklin, Louisiana. It was there, in one of those services, that we released the power of the Kingdom and declared that God wants you to have an abundant life. The following is a testimony sent to me via e-mail from my friend Jerry Jett, who dared to receive.

TWENTY-ONE-MILLION-DOLLAR ABUNDANT LIFE

Hello, Lemuel,

May our Lord richly bless you for the years of faithful service you have given to His Kingdom. You have crossed my mind many times since the days you held revivals for me in Franklin, LA.

At the close of one of those great revival services, you asked if anyone had something special they wanted from the Lord. Many came forward, and after the line emptied you surprisingly looked at me and asked if there was anything I wanted from the Lord. Sheepishly I said, "No, I have everything I need." You then added, "Isn't there something that you have always wanted?" I stuttered and slowly replied, "Well, I've always dreamed of having a few acres with horses on them." You then prayed for me and asked God to give me all that I dreamed of.

In the year that followed, the Lord began making it clear to me that my ministry in Franklin was coming to an end. While seeking the Lord for a sure word for my life, my brother and I started a marine transportation company for the Gulf of Mexico. Six years later we sold the company for twenty-one million dollars.

My son Clint, who was then my youth pastor, now pastors Victory Christian Center, a great church in Macon, GA, where I own sixteen beautiful acres with Appaloosa and Quarter horses on them.

Today my wife and I have been traveling the world, building churches for the poor and houses for poor pastors, caring for widows and orphans, helping kids go to college, as well as supporting missionaries.

Thanks for being my friend.

Jerry Jett

When you let God's words become Spirit and Life to you, you will instantly notice a turn toward abundant living. Suddenly your words will become weighty, powerful words of authority, with the power to fulfill dreams.

When Jesus spoke:

- The atmosphere changed
- He gave secrets proving his words have creative power
- The Holy Spirit released the Kingdom of Heaven in the lives of the people
- People were filled with excitement
- Miracles took place
- The Kingdom manifested, supplying wants, deliverance, and provision
- Demonic powers had to flee

THE IMPORTANCE OF THIS REVELATION

If we say what the Father is saying, the Holy Spirit is released; thus, the Kingdom of Heaven is manifested, making the economy, culture, morality, and blessings of the Kingdom available to us!

When people witness this manifestation, they suddenly develop an appetite for the things of the Kingdom. Before the manifestation they were interested only in their self-centered desires. But now, the words they hear have power and authority; there is hope; they are exhilarated with the joy of the Lord, and for some reason they now believe in miracles!

SO, TELL ME, HOW CAN I HEAR WHAT THE FATHER SAYS?

> Ephesians 5:18 (NLT): **Don't be drunk with wine, because that will ruin your life. Instead, *let the Holy Spirit fill and control you.*** [Emphasis added.]

> John 16:13 (KJV): **Howbeit when he, the Spirit of truth, is come, he will guide you into all truth: for he shall not speak of himself; but *whatsoever he shall hear, that shall he speak: and he will show you things to come.*** [Emphasis added.]

In order to hear the Father, we need to be filled with His Spirit—the Holy Spirit. God said the Holy Spirit would not speak just because He wants to say something. No! He only speaks when the Father gives Him something to say to us. And He only speaks what

He's heard the Father say. This is how you hear what the Father has said! Then the Father gives the Holy Spirit the right to show us our future.

This is huge! Do you want to know what your destiny is? Pay close attention to what Jesus says in John 4:46–53 (NIV):

> ... And there was a certain royal official whose son lay sick at Capernaum. When this man heard that Jesus had arrived in Galilee from Judea, he went to him and begged him to come and heal his son, who was close to death. "Unless you people see miraculous signs and wonders," Jesus told him, "you will never believe." The royal official said, "Sir, come down before my child dies." *Jesus replied, "You may go. Your son will live."* The man took Jesus at his word and departed. While he was still on the way, his servants met him with the news that his boy was living. When he inquired as to the time when his son got better, they said to him, "The fever left him yesterday at the seventh hour." Then the father realized that this was the exact time at which Jesus had said to him, "Your son will live." So he and his entire household believed. [Emphasis added.]

This is just one of many examples of the power of the spoken words of Jesus. When Jesus first declared in verse 50 "Your son will live," he didn't have to pray, cry, wail or beg. *He simply said,* "Your son will live"!

WHEN JESUS SPEAKS, CREATION IS RELEASED

Genesis 1:3 (KJV): **And God said, Let there be light: and there was light.**

Here we find the power of creation in the spoken word of the Almighty. Ten times in Genesis chapter 1 "God said" and creation took place.

What does this mean for you and me? When God speaks to us, His creative power is released into us. I believe that when we declare what He has said to us, His creative power and authority is then released into our environment.

Luke 5:12–13 (NIV): **While Jesus was in one of the towns, a man came along who was covered with leprosy. When he saw Jesus, he fell with his face to the ground and begged him, "Lord, if you are willing, you can make me clean." Jesus reached out his hand and touched the man. *"I am willing,"* he said. *"Be clean!" And immediately the leprosy left him.*** [Emphasis added.]

This leper asked the same question that many of us have asked of Jesus: "Lord, if you are willing ..." What did Jesus say? "I am willing." Then, with the power of the creative word, he said, "Be clean!" With those words, immediately the man was cleansed of the dreadful disease.

THE WORD CLEANS

> John 15:1-3 (NIV): **I am the true vine, and my Father is the gardener. He cuts off every branch in me that bears no fruit, while every branch that does bear fruit he prunes so that it will be even more fruitful. <u>You are already clean because of the word I have spoken to you.</u>** [Emphasis added.]

Please notice in verse 2 the word "prunes" and in verse 3 the word "clean." Both come from the same root word in the Greek, *katharos*. This word means "to purge, prune, or to make clean by purifying." Jesus explains, "Listen up! My Father is the gardener, and He prunes each believer. Yes, He cuts off everything that hinders and bears no fruit, and also prunes all who are producing so that they can and will produce much more." This is a law of the Kingdom that brings into existence in your life the multiplication of Kingdominion.

JESUS SAID, "IT'S ALL MINE, AND IT CAN ALL BE YOURS!"

> John 16:14-15 (NIV): **He [the Holy Spirit] will bring glory to me by taking from what is mine and making it known to you. <u>All that belongs to the Father is mine</u>. That is why *I said the Spirit will take from what is mine and make it known to you*.** [Emphasis added.]

Do you understand what this passage is saying? Jesus was saying, "Okay, here's the deal: I give my life for you; in turn, your inheritance as a child of God becomes all that is mine. That's right, everything Father God has belongs to me, and the plan is that the Holy Spirit will take from what is mine and give it to you!" *Wow! Wow! Wow!*

What does the Father have? He has everything! Look at the first word of John16:15: *all!* What part of *all* don't you understand? "*All* that the Father has," Jesus says; "It is *all* mine." Then He declares, **"That is why I said the Spirit will take from what is mine and make it known to you."**

Do you understand the implication? When the Holy Spirit brings what Jesus has been given by the Father and gives the same to you and you begin to use, declare and demonstrate, causing His power and purpose to be manifested here on earth, it brings Him (Jesus) glory!

"*All* that the Father has" means the treasure chest of Heaven; the government, economy, culture, morality, righteousness, peace, joy, love, health, etc., etc., etc. And Jesus says, "I have commissioned the Spirit of God to give it *all* to you"!

Thank you, Jesus! Allow me to ask you, was Jesus divine or human? The Word says in 2 Corinthians 8:9 (KJV), **"For ye know the grace of our Lord Jesus Christ, that, though he was rich, yet for your sakes he became poor, that ye through his poverty might be rich."**

What is the implication of this statement? Jesus stripped Himself of divinity. Yes, He chose to live not as God but as a human, like you and me. He did this in order to give us the Kingdom of Heaven, and by doing so He took on Himself our failures, faults, and sins—and in exchange, gave us grace and mercy.

"What is grace?" you might ask. **Grace is our receiving what Jesus deserved, and mercy is Jesus receiving what we deserved.**

We get Jesus' inheritance as a son from the Father. And as our elder brother, Jesus restores us to God's original plan, which is for us to rule as kings of the Earth.

Another important piece in the puzzle is that *Jesus said the Holy Spirit must dwell in you.* You see, the Holy Spirit had been with the disciples but had not been *in* the disciples.

John 16:7 (KJV): **Nevertheless I tell you the truth; It is expedient for you that I go away: for if I go not away, the Comforter [the Holy Spirit] will not come unto you; but if I depart,** *I will send him unto you.* [Emphasis added.]

Jesus is saying, "When the Holy Spirit dwells in you, He will declare unto you what is Mine!"

There is a big difference between being "with you" and being "in you." When the Holy Spirit is *in you*, the exact same thing Jesus said in John 6:63, concerning His words, will also happen for you: "My words are Spirit [the Holy Spirit] and Life." Then when you make your powerful declaration in faith because you heard the Father speak, that is when the Holy Spirit takes your words on its wings, searching for an open heart. When found, the Spirit places your words of power into the open hearts of men, women, and children, releasing the creative power of Kingdominion!

I think the thing for us to remember is that Jesus did no mighty works until the Holy Spirit descended upon Him and remained. This happened immediately after his cousin John had baptized Him in water. Look at John's recollection of this great event:

> John 1:32 (NIV): **Then John gave this testimony: "I saw the Spirit come down from heaven as a dove and remain on him."**

Last week, while sitting in my office writing portions of this book, I looked out the window, and there in my yard were, I estimate, seventy to a hundred cardinals—also known as "redbirds." I had never seen anything quite like it, and there they were, right outside of my window, on the ground. Every so often, they would fly into the trees, but they would quickly return to the ground in front of me. I called for my wife, DaVonne, and the two of us marveled at this awesome display. I said to DaVonne, "There has to be some significance to this." I began to ask God what He was showing me.

I began to research the word "cardinal" and found this incredible definition: A cardinal is a high ecclesiastical official who ranks next below the Pope and is appointed by him to assist him. [Merriam-Webster © 2011]

Jesus is our High Priest, and He is showing us constantly, through signs and wonders, that it is His will for us to be a Cardinal in the Kingdom of God—someone with supernatural power and authority; yes, a priest, here on Earth.

Revelations 1:5-6 (KJV): **And from Jesus Christ, who is the faithful witness, and the first begotten of the dead, and the prince of the *kings of the earth*. Unto him that loved us, and washed us from our sins in his own blood, 6 And hath made us kings and *priests unto God and his Father*; to him be glory and dominion for ever and ever. Amen.** [Emphasis added.]

The red color of the red bird [cardinal] symbolizes the Holy Spirit; this is the liturgical color of the feast of Pentecost. Red also represents fire and is associated with power and importance. Crimson red also symbolizes the presence of God.

When I saw all the cardinals in my yard, I knew it had to be a God thing—and indeed it was.

WHAT WERE THE LAST WORDS JESUS SAID TO HIS DISCIPLES?

Luke 24:49 (KJV): **And, behold, I send the promise of my Father upon you: but tarry ye in the city of Jerusalem, *until ye be endued with power from on high.*** [Emphasis added.]

We need the power of the Holy Spirit in our lives so that we can hear what the Father wants to say and see what the Father wants us to do. Then and only then can we become His cardinals—priests here on Earth!

This past Sunday, I went into my office to pray and prepare for the morning service. I looked out the window, hoping to see the cardinals. As if on cue, two doves flew down and landed right outside my window. Immediately the Father, through the Holy Spirit, said to me, "The first dove represents the first time the Holy Spirit came and remained. The other dove represents that He—the Holy Spirit—and *all* that Jesus has is given to you as well!"

> John 1:32 (NIV): **Then John gave this testimony: "I saw <u>the Spirit come down from heaven as a dove and remain on him.</u>** [Emphasis added.]

Please notice the words "**and remain on him**." Who does the Holy Spirit submit to? The Father! John said the Spirit remained on Jesus. Because the Spirit remained on Him, He had continuing contact with what the Father was saying and what the Father was doing. Thus, all who came to Jesus were healed. Yes, their Bailout was provided!

My friend Pastor Arthur Smith, before he went home to be with the Lord, loved to raise white doves. He raised doves because of his love for the Holy Spirit—doves being symbols of the Spirit. Brother Arthur explained to me many things about doves that I found extremely interesting. One of the things he told me was that doves are monogamous. This represents the purity and submission of the Holy Spirit to God, our Father. I think that is why God the Father chose a dove to represent His Holy Spirit.

Have you ever really watched a dove, or held one? They are so gentle and have beautifully innocent eyes.

They are easily put to flight because of their being very sensitive to trouble or danger in their environment.

I heard a great man of God, Bill Johnson, use the following illustration that pierced my heart! He said, "If you have a dove sitting on your shoulder and you want him to remain, every step you take will be with the dove in mind!"

Jesus Himself commands believers, His disciples, to be filled with the Holy Spirit—thus, to be endued with supernatural power. Power to prosper, power to pray, power to believe, power to heal and be healed, power of deliverance, power to operate in the nine gifts of the Spirit (1 Corinthians 12:6-11), power to overcome sin, power to heal the brokenhearted, power to raise the dead, and power to give to others what has been given to you!If there is an arena in your life in which a Bailout from God is needed, the best way to receive what the Kingdom of Heaven provides is to do what the Father does and speak what you hear the Father say. This produces in you the perfect will of the Father for your life. But how, is the question. One way is to study the word of God and pray the Holy Spirit will give you wisdom and understanding. When you begin to believe the word, the Holy Spirit will give you power to do what you are hearing God's Word say to you. However, you can hear what the Father says, and do what He does, another way.

BENEFITS OF BEING FILLED WITH THE SPIRIT

Twelve years ago, while in Germany, I had a near death experience. So weak that I could not get out of the hospital bed, I knew I was fading fast. The doctors had no clue what was happening to me, and I was desperate for help. I asked my wife to call home and tell our family—my mother, brothers, and sister, and our children.

Now, my family are all filled with the Holy Spirit and daily pray in the Spirit, which means they pray in a Heavenly language, a language that Satan cannot understand nor interfere with. When the enemy does not know what is being said, this is of great benefit to your prayer life. I know this sounds crazy to those who have never experienced something like this, but believe me if you can, it is more than real.

Another benefit is, the Word of God teaches us that the Holy Spirit knows how to pray when we do not. My family were thousands of miles away and had very little information. The doctors had no clue. How, then, should they pray?

As my family began to pray, they started to allow the Spirit of God to pray through them. Suddenly my brother Troy began to see in the Spirit. Please remember John 16:13 (KJV), which states,

> **Howbeit when he, the Spirit of truth, is come, he will guide you into all truth: for he shall not speak of himself; but whatsoever he shall hear, that shall he speak: and *he will show you things to come.*** [Emphasis added.]

The Holy Spirit showed my brother, from thousands of miles away, the spirit of death in the form of an evil darkness over me as I lay in the hospital room. He even described the room I was in, he saw so clearly in the Spirit. Troy said that as he prayed in tongues (the prayer language of the Spirit), he noticed his prayer language getting more intense, and the spirit of death began to lift off of me. After several minutes the spirit of death left the room.

"Wait a minute," you may be saying. "You said the enemy does not understand this so-called prayer language. So how did the spirit of death know to leave?"

Psalm 91:11 (KJV): **For he shall give his angels charge over thee, to keep thee in all thy ways.**

Hebrews 1:14 (NIV): **Are not all angels ministering spirits sent to serve those who will inherit salvation?**

Although there are many things hidden that I personally do not have all the revelation about, I will speculate. I believe that as my brother prayed in the Spirit, the Holy Spirit was praying to God the Father, who then sent one of His warring angels to that hospital room where I lay. With the authority and power of the Sovereign Lord, the angel declared that the spirit of death had to *Leave!* And leave he did! Hallelujah! The next day I flew home, and I have been well ever since.

You do not have to believe me, but please be open to find out for yourself. God always has more for us, and the Holy Spirit is where the "more" comes from. If you are open to simply trust God to give you what you need, please do not place restrictions on the Father who loves you enough to give the life of His only Son. It is this Son who said,

John 16:7 (KJV): **Nevertheless I tell you the truth; It is expedient for you that I go away: for if I go not away , the Comforter [the Holy Spirit] will not come unto you; but if I depart, *I will send him unto you.*** [Emphasis added.]

PRAYER TO RECEIVE THE HOLY SPIRIT

Heavenly Father, my most Holy God, I humbly ask you to forgive me of my unbelief and my sins. Wash me clean with the precious blood of Jesus, and sanctify me, set me apart from wrong patterns of thinking and teaching.

I desire to have everything You have for me, and I realize that Jesus, Your only begotten Son, commanded His followers to receive His gift, the Holy Spirit.

There are many things I do not understand, but I believe You are a loving God who has my best interest at heart. Because of this, I believe You want me to have Your best. It is my desire to be filled to overflowing with the empowerment of Your Holy Spirit. Jesus, my Savior and King, baptize me in the Holy Spirit so that the power of Your resurrection will work in me and transform me according to Your will.

Father, please give the gifts of your Spirit to me, allowing them to work through me so that Your kingdom may be manifested in my life. I ask this in Jesus' mighty name. Amen!

Now, if you truly mean what you prayed, begin to praise the Lord out loud, in an audible voice. If words come to mind that you do not know or understand, simply speak them in faith. Remember, the Holy Spirit is a perfect gentleman, and He will never embarrass you or cause you to do anything that will shame you, your family, your church, or your country. He loves you, and He wants to talk to you and through you.

If you have no evidence of your prayer language, do not lose heart. He comes differently to all, never having to duplicate Himself. I have friends who received Him instantly, while others were filled while driving down the road—and some even awaken from sleep praying in a Heavenly language. So never tell God how; just be open!

IN CONCLUSION

AFTER you speak your first words of your own prayer language, Satan will probably tell you that what just happened was not real. He'll say things like, "You're just making up these words that sound like gibberish." Let me encourage you to realize that Satan does not want you to receive the Holy Spirit, because he knows it is the Holy Spirit that gave Jesus the power and authority to resist his temptations (Luke 4:1–13), and if you receive the Spirit, Satan knows that you will have the same power.

This is indeed real! Do not allow the enemy to lie to you and keep you from receiving! I have seen the dead raised to life five times, and each time I was praying in the Spirit! The Holy Spirit is the teacher of the "Principles of Kingdominion," and when you are baptized in His power, you have the most important Bailout!

Kingdominion Titles from
Lemuel David Miller

God's Bailout
In Times of Recession
Learn how to get God's Bailout for your life in three arenas:
Supplying your wants—Getting your secret desires.
Deliverance—God wants to bail you out from your mistakes and failures.
Provision—God will provide in every area of your life.

God's Bailout
Principles of Kingdominion
Ready to receive the power and authority that Jesus promised you? This book will teach you how to have what we call "Kingdominion," which is the dominion to rule, manage, and multiply the resources of the Kingdom of Heaven here on Earth.

God's Bailout
Help from Another World
In this book you will learn that nothing is impossible. Learn how to rule and dominate your environment, heal the sick, declare wealth, and watch God's divine health and prosperity come to your life and household.